Frank Doll

Mastering the Fretboard

Frank Doll

Mastering the Fretboard

Harmonics, Fretboard – Knowledge, Scales and Chords for Guitarists

ED 22592
ISBN 978-3-7957-1060-6
ISMN 979-0-001-16133-6
UPC 841886028340

www.schott-music.com

Translation: Ingrid Baumann
Editors: Julia Baldauf, Rebecca Castle, Clifford Caesar, Helmut Kagerer, Stefan Weber
Cover: Peter Klein
Cover photography: © chesterF – Fotolia.com
Layout: Stefan Weis, Mainz-Kastel

ED 22592
ISBN 978-3-7957-1060-6
ISMN 979-0-001-16133-6
UPC 841886028340
Printed in Germany · BSS 57623

Preface

The market is well-stocked with great books about guitar licks, guitar riffs, guitar related stuff, books with fingering charts and literature about harmony. Still, what's missing is, in my opinion, a concept which explains theory and relates it to guitar–orientated practice. How do you transfer music theory to the fretboard? How do you move quickly between major and minor chords? Are not melodies sequences of notes based on tonality? Of course they are, but often they are played without an understanding of the relationship. Songs which might even be structured identically often have to be practiced anew.

Mastering the Fretboard aims to solve this problem. The book focusses on the fretboard and provides a logical approach to it. Starting with intervals and their positions on the fretboard, my interval notation for the fingering diagrams are easily adapted to every key. I also include practical exercises in guitar related topics like Drop2–Voicings.

This book is for all guitar players looking for new sounds and acoustic patterns after years of playing pentatonic, open chords and bar chords. It offers new perspectives for guitarists who have been playing by notes and tabs since the beginning of their careers.

Mastering the Fretboard is a supplement to books about music theory, but does not replace them. It is designed to provide you with tips, to explain connections, and to be a practical inspiration for creative use. This book can be used in instrumental lessons, but is also suitable for self–study.

Have fun reading, learning, practising and performing!

Frank Doll

P.S.: I look forward to receiving your questions and comments! Please send your message to info@schott–music.com; and it will be forwarded to me.

Contents

Introduction

In contrast to keyboard instruments, where the notes within one octave can be easily identified via the black and white keys, it is considerably harder to locate notes on a guitar. Apart from the dots on the 3rd, 5th, 7th and 9th fret, and the double marks on the 12th fret which highlight the octave of the open strings, there are no reference points. A semitone step upwards on the fretboard requires a horizontal move covering one fret in the direction of the body. A whole step consists of two half steps and therefore needs to be produced by moving two frets forward on the fretboard. In figure 1, the individual notes of the C major scale are displayed, showing their position on the six strings and their distribution up to the 12th fret. Please keep in mind that there is only a semitone step between the notes e and f, as well as between b and c', respectively.

[Figure 1: Position of the notes on the fretboard up to the 12th fret]

```
e'  ─f'────────g'────────a'────────b'──c''────────d''────────e''
b   ─c'────────d'────────e'──f'────────g'────────a'────────b'
g   ────a────────b──c'────────d'────────e'──f'────────g'
d   ────e──f────────g────────a────────b──c'────────d'
A   ──B──c────────d────────e──f────────g────────a
E   ─F────────G────────A────────B──c────────d────────e
```

The notes between the whole steps, for example between the notes f and g, will not be considered as yet.

The different octave ranges are indicated by capitalization, lower case, and lower case with a dash. Notes written in the same way have identical pitch ranges.

There are two options for learning the notes on your six strings:

Option 1: Memorize all notes on the fretboard – a huge effort.

Option 2: Learn the notes of the E– and A–string and understand the fretboard's system. Welcome to the Mastering the Fretboard approach. Step by step, we will assemble intervals and chords and make the fretboard more accessible. We'll start with octaves.

CHAPTER 1 Octave Positions

We divide the fretboard horizontally into five positions. A position defines the locations of a note's octaves in relation to each other. As a starting point, I've chosen the note e, which is located on the two outer strings.

[Figure 2: The note e and its octaves on the fretboard up to the 12ᵗʰ fret]

Here you can see the five positions of the note e. In order to determine the position, we apply the following rules:

Position 1:
When a note lies on fret x on the E–string, its 2ⁿᵈ octave also lies on fret x on the e'–string.
The 1ˢᵗ octave lies on the d–string on fret x plus 2 (x+2).
Here, the x represents a placeholder for any fret and is used as in the following example: the note F lies on the E–string on the 1ˢᵗ fret, which means that the octave f lies on the d–string on the 3ʳᵈ fret. As you can see, it's easy maths. Let's move on to the formulas for the next positions.

Position 2:
When a note lies on the d–string on fret x, its 1ˢᵗ octave lies on the b–string on fret x plus 3 (x+3).

Position 3:
When a note lies on the A–string on fret x, its 1ˢᵗ octave lies on the b–string on fret x minus 2 (x–2). We can therefore determine a note on the b–string via position 2 and position 3.

Position 4:
When a note lies on the A–string on fret x, its 1ˢᵗ octave lies on the g–string on fret x plus 2 (x+2).

Position 5:
When a note lies on the E–string on fret x, its 1ˢᵗ octave lies on the g–string on fret x minus 3 (x–3). Its 2ⁿᵈ octave lies on the e'–string on fret x, respectively.

The notes of the g–string can be determined either via the E–string (position 5) or via the A–string (position 4).

In the next figure, the numeral 1 shows the position of any optional note. Accordingly, [1'] shows its 1st octave, [1''] its second octave.

[Figure 3: Notes and their octaves – position 1 to 4]

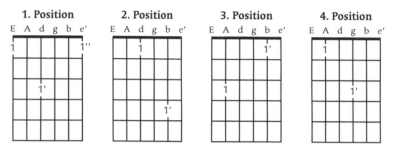

[Figure 4: Notes and octaves of position 5]

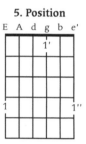

'**Position**' is an important term for the method of this book, as the classification of intervals, arpeggios, and scales is based on the system of the five aforementioned positions. A position is defined by the place of the keynote on a string and the resulting positions of its octaves. With the help of the five positions, we are able to determine a keynote and its octaves in a certain fretboard area in both directions. While playing, I consider the fretboard and the positions in two ways:

Progressive: I play upwards, which means into the direction of the guitar's body.
Regressive: I play downwards, which means into the direction of the guitar's head.

When I find myself in position 1 (keynote on the E–string), my way of playing is progressive, that is upwards, up to the keynote's octave on the d–string (x+2). Now I can decide whether I want to change to position 2 and keep playing progressively there, or whether, starting from the octave, I rather want to stay in position 1 and play regressively to the 2nd octave on the e'–string.

Generally, I recommend the following division:

1. Progressive:
Position 1: Keynote up to 1st octave
Position 2: Keynote up to 1st octave
Position 3: 1st octave up to the highest possible note of the position on the e'–string
Position 4: Keynote up to 1st octave
Position 5: 1st octave up to 2nd octave

2. Regressive:
Position 1: 1st octave up to 2nd octave
Position 2: 1st octave up to the highest possible note of the position on the e'–string
Position 3: Keynote up to 1st octave
Position 4: 1st octave up to the highest possible note of the position on the e'–string
Position 5: Keynote up to 1st octave

When playing progressively, my fingering starts with the index or the middle finger, depending on the tonal material. When playing regressively, my fingering starts with the ring finger or the little finger, again depending on the musical situation. If you are unsure at any point when working through the book, I recommend revisiting this instruction.

Here are some further examples of this system. Of course, we seldom start with position 1, as the starting note is on the E–string. As the note c lies on the E–string on the 8th fret, the tonal possibilities of the first seven frets would stay unexploited if we started from position 1. The following examples show the remaining notes of the open strings and their octaves.

[Figure 5: The note a and its octaves on the fretboard up to the 12th fret]

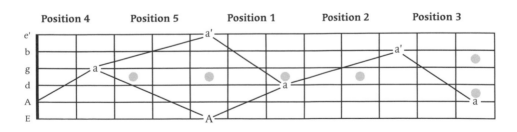

For the note a, we start on the A–string and so apply the rule for position 4. We then move on to position 1 over position 5 followed by positions 2 and 3.

[Figure 6: The note d and its octaves on the fretboard up to the 12ᵗʰ fret]

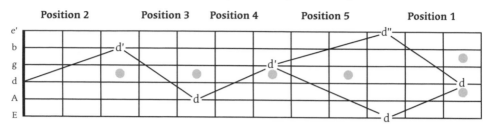

[Figure 7: The note g and its octaves on the fretboard up to the 12ᵗʰ fret]

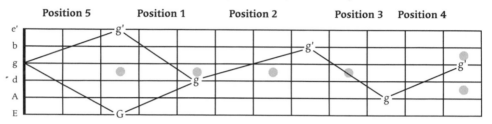

[Figure 8: The note b and its octaves on the fretboard up to the 12ᵗʰ fret]

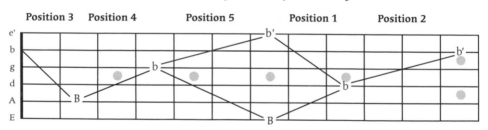

This system of five positions works with all 12 notes. Determine the note or its position in the front part of the fretboard. Then, apply the formulas for the following positions. Attention: for all notes which are not located on open strings, the positions will lead beyond the 12ᵗʰ fret.

Next, an example of the note c. To play the note c on the lower part of the fretboard (near the head of the guitar), apply the 1ˢᵗ fret on the b–string. Consequently, position 3 is applied first. As soon as all five positions have been applied, we reach the note c'' on the 13ᵗʰ fret on the b–string.

I am going to present some ways to train your tonal overview of the fretboard. Please integrate these exercises into your daily practice. It is not enough to have read the instructions …

Exercise 1

Determine a sequence of notes. For your orientation, I propose the following order:

C – G – D – A – E – B – F#/G♭ – D♭ – A♭ – E♭ – B♭ – F

Explanation: Notes with a '#' accidental have to be played one fret higher than usual, as the starting note is one semitone sharp. Accordingly, notes with a '♭' accidental have to be played one fret lower, as the starting note is one semitone flat.

➪ Determine the first position of the note c and play all octaves in this position.

➪ Change to the note g. Determine the first position and play all octaves of this position.

➪ Follow the order of the notes and determine the first position for each note.

When you are able to determine the first position for all these notes, practice this exercise applying to position 2. Afterwards, study positions 3 to 5, one after the other.

Exercise 2

Only start practising exercise 2 when you have mastered exercise 1. You can use the sequence of notes from exercise 1.

➪ Determine the first possible position on the fretboard. For the note c, this is position 3. Play all octaves of this position.

➪ Now, determine the following positions of the note c and play the octaves.

➪ Apply this exercise to the whole fretboard.

➪ Then, start with the next note and repeat the exercise.

Exercise 3

Determine a certain area of the fretboard, for example from the open strings up to the 4th fret. You can use the sequence of notes from exercise 1.

➪ Determine the position of the note c, which is position 3 here, and play the octaves.

➪ In this area, determine the position of g, which is position 5 here, and play the octaves.

➪ Determine the positions of the following notes in this fretboard area and play their octaves.

➪ Define the nearest possible fretboard area using the note c. Therefore, start with position 4.

➪ Repeat this exercise for all notes in the new fretboard area.

↪ Repeat this exercise for all starting positions of c and determine the positions of the other notes originating from there.

As this exercise is quite time-consuming initially, it is sufficient to practice only one fretboard area a day. As soon as you feel more confident, you can increase the number of fretboard areas per day.

Exercise 4
The following exercise was coined by Joe Satriani and is called 'Finding the Note'[1]. Here you can train your skills on a certain note. Set your metronome to 60 bpm.

↪ Determine a note, for example, c on all six strings on the fretboard area between the open strings and the 12th fret.
↪ Start playing on the E–string on beat 1. On the next beat, play the note on the A–string. Alternate the strings on each beat.
↪ Once you have reached the e'–string, turn around and play the exercise backwards down to the low E–string.
↪ Practice each note for three minutes continuously.

Should you feel overstrained by the fast pace, try this exercise without the metronome. Should you feel insufficiently challenged, increase the tempo.

Exercise 5
This exercise was devised by the German guitarist, Abi von Reininghaus, and is divided into three degrees of difficulty. In order to control the location of the notes on the fretboard, three questions can be used as a guideline. For each question, fill in your answers.

Easy exercise: On which fret lies note 'x' on string 'y'?
For example: 'on which fret lies the note a on the d–string?' Answer: 'on the 7th fret.'

Well then, on which fret lies the note ...
... a on the d–string?
... e on the g–string?
... d on the b–string?
... c on the E–string?

A little bit more demanding: Which note lies on string x on fret y?

---

[1] Joe Satriani, 'Finding the Note' in: Guitar for the Practicing Musician, Vol. 11/1987, Joe Satriani Guitar Secrets, 1993 Cherry Lane Music Company

For example: 'which note lies on the d–string on the 2nd fret?' – Answer: 'the note e.'

Which note lies on the string...
... d on fret 5?
... E on fret 3?
... A on fret 10?
... g on fret 5?

Difficult exercise: On which string lies note x on fret y?
For example: 'on which string lies the note a on the 2nd fret?' – Answer: 'on the g–string.' Be careful, as in this exercise not every question leads to an answer! For example, to ask for the string of the note f on the 2nd fret is pointless.

On which string lies the note...
... a on fret 2?
... d on fret 5?
... e on fret 6?
... b on fret 4?

These exercises could be made into a kind of quiz for guitarists and are a great way of testing your knowledge. Come up with your own questions, write them down, and find the answers yourself.

I hope you have a clear understanding of the system of the fretboard. Please take your time practicing the material carefully, as it will greatly help you developing your skills.

CHAPTER 2

Basic Elements – Thirds

In this chapter, we will treat the basic elements of music: the thirds. We start with the third of the note c, which is the note e. So, we skip the note d, the second. There are two kinds of thirds: major thirds and minor thirds. The major third (short: 3) is located four semitones from the root; the minor third (short: ♭3) only contains three semitones. In this book, I will use the term 'semitones' as you can easily trace the intervals on the frets of your guitar. One semitone upwards means moving one fret higher.

Let's have a look at the thirds of the C major scale. In each major scale, the semitone steps are located between the 3rd/4th and the 7th/8th tones. The remaining steps are whole tones. In figure 9, you can see the C major scale horizontally on the fretboard, starting on the 3rd fret of the A–string.

[Figure 9: C major on the A–string, horizontally]

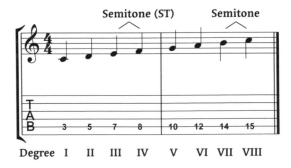

So, the semitone steps of the C major scale are located between the notes e/f and b/c, respectively. The degree notation (I, II, III, and so on) is going to be important in the following chapters.

Let's have a look at the diatonic thirds. 'Diatonic' means that we are moving within a specific key, which is the C major scale in this case. This appendix is important, because for each note, a major as well as a minor third can be built:

Between the notes c and e, there are 4 semitones, which means that e is the major third of c. Between the notes d and f, there are 3 semitones, which means that f is the minor third of d. Between the notes e and g, there are 3 semitones, which means that g is the minor third of e, and so on.

After having played through the whole scale and having built thirds upon each diatonic note, you will have noticed that the major thirds originate on degrees I, IV, and V, the minor thirds on degrees II, III, VI, and VII. See figure 10 to find the root and the corresponding diatonic third of the C major scale.

[Figure 10: The diatonic thirds of the major scale – example: C major]

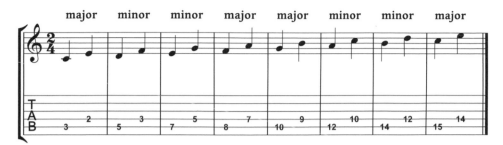

- **Note:** the major thirds are located on the next string one fret lower (fret x – 1) than the starting note. Correspondingly, the minor thirds are located on the next string two frets lower (fret x – 2) than the starting note.

In some of the following chapters, it is advisable to play the minor third on the same string, three frets higher than the starting note (see figure 13). Likewise, you can play the major third on the string of the starting note, moving up four frets.

The only exception is the case where the starting note lies on the g–string. Let's have a look at the A major scale on the g–string in figure 11.

[Figure 11: A major horizontally on the g–string]

- **Note:** Between the g– and the b– string, there is a naturally-tuned major third. This is why we can play the major third in the same fret on the b–string (fret x). For the minor third, we move one fret down from the starting note (fret x – 1) on the b–string.

[Figure 12: The position of the major thirds (3) on the fretboard]

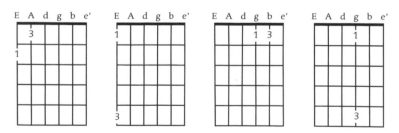

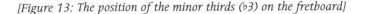

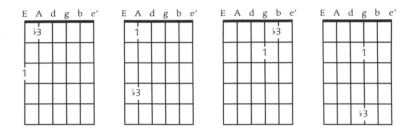

[Figure 14: The diatonic thirds on the g– and b–strings in A major]

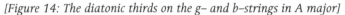

Thirds are the most important elements for the construction of chords and arpeggios. The third is also perfectly suited to harmonizing melodies, for example, to play it polyphonically in two or more voices.

Exercise:
For this exercise, please use the following keys and starting notes:
C major (A–string 3rd fret / g–string 5th fret / b–string 1st fret)
G major (E–string 3rd fret / d–string 5th fret)
D major (A–string 5th fret / b–string 3rd fret)
A major (E–string 5th fret / g–string 2nd fret)
E major (d–string 2nd fret / b–string 5th fret)
B major (A–string 2nd fret / g–string 4th fret)
F major (E–string 1st fret / d–string 3rd fret / b–string 6th fret)

↻ Play the major scale upwards and downwards horizontally on one string, starting from the root. Don't forget to play the semitone steps between the 3rd and 4th and the 7th and 8th notes.
↻ Repeat the scale and add the diatonic thirds (see figures 10 and 14). Please pay attention to the correct sequence of the thirds, which is major – minor – minor – major – major – minor – minor – major.

CHAPTER 3

The Sound of Rock – The Fifth

In this chapter we will cover fifths. The note g is the fifth note of the root c, so g is the fifth of c. When starting from the note d, the 5th note is a; when starting from e, the 5th note is b, and so on. The fifth is part of the group of 'perfect' intervals, together with the prime, fourth, and octave, for which there are no major or minor equivalents.

In interval notation, the fifth is represented by the number 5. If a fifth is increased by a semitone, we speak of an augmented fifth and write '#5'. If a fifth is flattened by a semitone, a diminished fifth results, which is written as 'b5'.

As we count the semitone steps between the notes c and g, we get seven steps. A perfect fifth counts seven steps, an augmented fifth counts eight, and a diminished fifth counts six semitone steps upwards. The term 'upwards' means that we consider the scale to be rising in pitch. Let's have a look at the note c and its fifth g regarding their positions relative to each other on the fretboard.

[Figure 15: The root c and its fifth g over two strings]

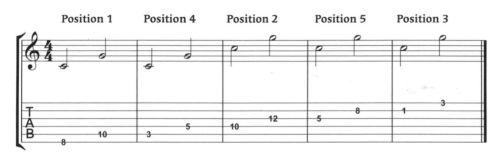

In the positions 5 and 3 (measures 4 and 5), the root is represented in the octave of the corresponding position. You can see that the fifth is located on the next string, two frets higher. An exception can again be found between the g– and the b–strings, where the fifth is located three frets higher.

■ **Note:** With roots on the E–, A–, d–, and b–strings, the fifth of a note is located on the next string two frets higher (fret x+2). If the root lies on the g–string, you can find its fifth on the b–string three frets higher (fret x+3) on the next string.

But this is only half the truth, as the same notes can be played on different strings (see chapter 1). Now have a look at figure 16, which shows the position of fifths two strings away.

[Figure 16: The root c and its fith g over three strings]

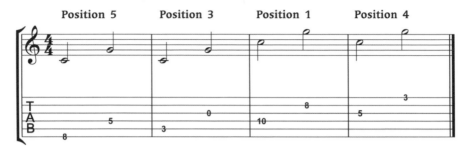

Due to the number of strings, only four positions can be demonstrated here.

■ Note: Starting from the E– or A– strings you will find the fifth two strings higher and three frets lower (fret x–3).
If the root lies on the d– or g– string, the fifth is positioned two strings higher and two frets lower (fret x–2).

[Figure 17: The position of the fifths on the fretboard]

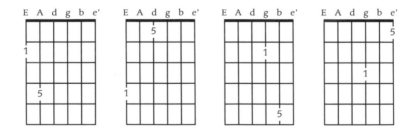

In rock and heavy metal music, the fifth is an important interval as the so-called 'power chord' stems from the consonance of the root and the fifth. By using distorted guitar sounds, power chords sound better than conventional triads.

Figure 18 shows the position of power chords on the fretboard. The labels E–type, A–type, d–type and g–type define the string of the root. The root gets the interval label 1, the fifth gets the label 5. The octave of the root gets marked with 1 again. The correct designation of the octave would be 1', but often the fifth is the lowest note of the power chord. This is why we will do without such labeling. In the chord names, power chords get the abbreviation '5'. A C5 is therefore a power chord with the root c, a G5 power chord has the root g, and so on.

[Figure 18: Power chords with roots on the E–, A–, d–, and g– String.]

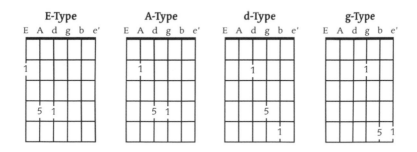

Figure 19 shows the four types of power chords, using the example of a C5 chord. The position which carries the root on the b–string is left out here because it is used extremely rarely. However, it can be built just like the power chords on the E–, A–, and d– strings.

[Figure 19: The 4 types of the C5 chord]

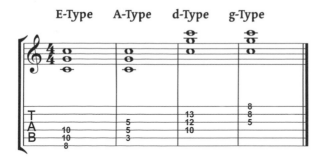

In the following example, you see a guitar riff from the song Fear of the Dark by the band, Iron Maiden. Prime and fifth of the chords are played alternately in a 16th note pattern.

[Figure 20: Iron Maiden: "Fear of the Dark"]

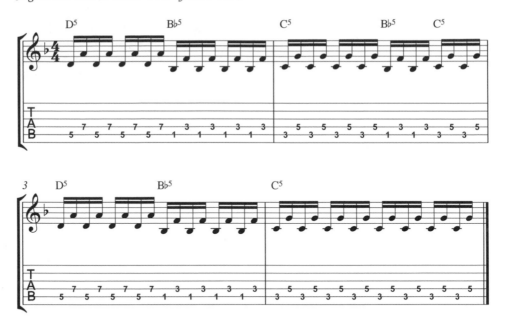

In the last few decades, the so–called 'Drop D' tuning has become popular, enabling guitarists to play power chords with even more sonority. However, it is not easy to tune down typical rock guitars with free–floating vibrato devices to D (drop D) without completely putting them out of tune. Check out the following trick if you want to thicken your power chords: simply double the fifth on the string below the root, and it will sound much more powerful.

[Figure 21: Power chords with doubled fifth in the bass by the example of C5]

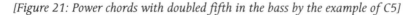

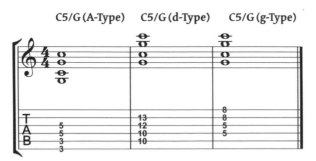

In order to illustrate this, see the riff below from the song Last Resort by the metal band Papa Roach.

[Figure 22: Papa Roach: "Last Resort"]

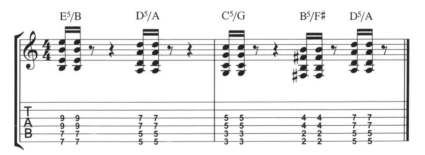

Let's have a look at the interval of the diminished fifth. As previously explained, a diminished fifth is built by flattening the fifth by a semitone.

[Figure 23: The root c and its rising diminished fifth g♭ (♭5)]

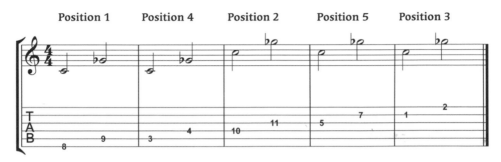

■ **Note:** If the root lies on the E–, A–, d–, or b– string, its diminished fifth (♭5) is positioned one fret higher on the next string (fret x+1). If the root lies on the g– string, its diminished fifth lies two frets higher on the b– string (fret x+2).

In the next figure, you can see the diminished fifths distributed over three strings.

[Figure 24: The root c and its diminished fifth g♭ over three strings]

■ **Note:** If the root lies on the E– or A– string, its diminished fifth is positioned four frets lower and two strings away (fret x–4). However, if the root lies on the d– or g– string, its diminished fifth is positioned three frets lower, two strings away (fret x–3).

[Figure 25: The position of the diminished fifths (♭5) on the fretboard]

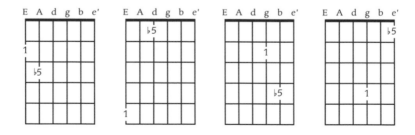

In pop music, the augmented fifth is rarely to be found. In order to get an augmented fifth (♯5), you have to increase the fifth by a semitone. Figure 26 shows the note c and its augmented fifth g♯ (♯5) distributed on neighboring strings.

[Figure 26: The root c and its augmented fifth g♯ (♯5) on two strings]

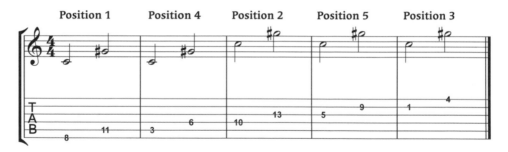

■ **Note:** If the root lies on the E–, A–, d–, or b– string, its augmented fifth is positioned three frets higher on the next string (fret x+3). If the root lies on the g–string, its augmented fifth is positioned four frets higher on the b– string (fret x+4).

Of course, the augmented fifth can also be played two strings from the root.

[Figure 27: The root c and its augmented fifth g♯ distributed over three strings]

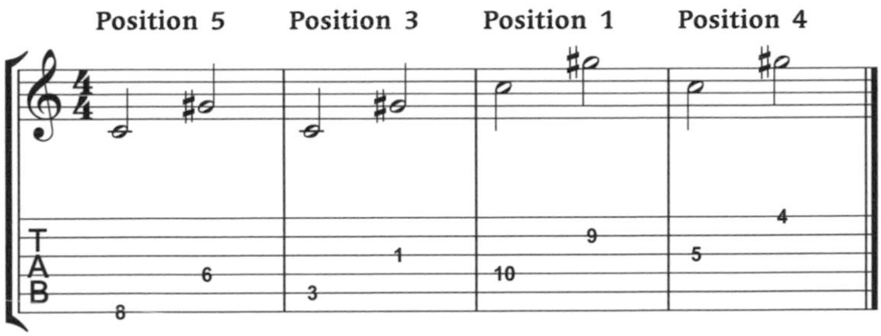

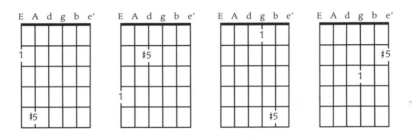

■ **Note:** If the root lies on the E– or A– string, its augmented fifth lies two strings away and two frets lower (fret x–2). If the root lies on the d– or g-string, its augmented fifth lies two strings away and one fret lower (fret x–1).

[Figure 28: Position of the augmented fifth (♯5) on the fretboard]

In any case, make sure you memorize the positions of the perfect fifths in relation to the root. You can derive these with your knowledge of diminished and augmented fifths.

CHAPTER 4

Triads and Arpeggios

4.1. The Major Triad

Having studied power chords, we are now going to have a look at the first 'real' chords and arpeggios, which are the triads. A chord is, in its most simple form, a layering of thirds. Depending on the order in which we stack major and minor thirds, a certain chord type, for example major or minor, results.

Now, starting again with C major with the root c. This time we add two diatonic thirds: first e and then g. This layering of thirds results in a major third from c to e (4 semitones) and in a minor third from e to g (3 semitones). This chord type is called a 'major chord'. In chord notation however, you do not have to add the word 'major'. The capital letter of the chord's root is enough, for example: C, G, D.

Note	Interval	Note	Interval	Note	Chord Type
c	major third	e	minor third	g	C major
Root		Third		Fifth	

Or, to put it simply:

Major third + minor third = major chord.

Some confusion might arise with the label 'third' because it can have two meanings. The term may be used to designate the interval of a third, namely the distance of three or four semitones between two notes. The note in the middle of a major chord in root position is also called the third.

Figure 29 shows how C major triads in root position are distributed on two strings, and where the root is located. When you play the notes of a chord successively, you get a broken triad, or 'arpeggio'. In an arpeggio, the notes of a chord are played successively without blending into each other.

In the following examples, you can see the function of each individual note and their position in the arpeggio. The 'function' describes the relation of a note to the root, that is, the role a note takes within a chord. Here, the interval abbreviations are used again:

1= root
3= major third
♭3= minor third
5= fifth
♭5= diminished fifth
#5= augmented fifth

[Figure 29: C major arpeggios over two strings]

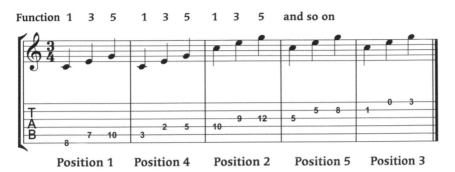

Of course, you do not have to keep the [¾] time. Choose any note value: 8th notes, 8th note triplets, 16th notes, and try the exercise again. Also practise the other way round, starting from the highest note and descending from there. In addition, make sure to vary the root! You can use the sequences of notes we used in exercise 1, chapter 1. Practice the changes very slowly at first.

You might have wondered how your favorite guitar players are able to master their solos and fills within so many different octaves with the greatest of ease. Here, I have an exercise for you. It's a G major triad, starting in position 1.

[Figure 30: G major triad over three octaves]

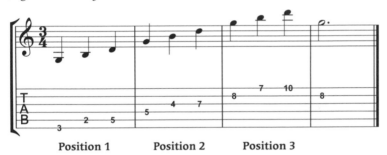

Of course, you do not have to keep the [¾] time. Choose any note value: 8th notes, 8th note triplets, 16th notes, and try the exercise again. Also practise the other way round, starting from the highest note and descending from there. In addition, make sure to vary the root! You can use the sequences of notes we used in exercise 1, chapter 1. Practice the changes very slowly at first.

In figures 31 and 32, I have created two exercises and possible lines with this longform arpeggio. Figure 31 is based on groups of three, which are to be practiced as 8th note triplets. Try to play this exercise with 16th notes too. Figure 32 shows the arpeggio, structured in 16th notes. Due to the rhythmic shift, this line sounds very dynamic. Try to integrate hammer–ons and pull–offs!

[Figure 31: G major longform arpeggio in triplets]

[Figure 32: G major longform arpeggio in sixteenth notes]

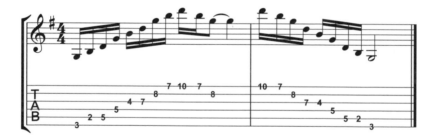

Here's another line, this time in D major, starting in position 4.

[Figure 33: D major arpeggio over 2 octaves]

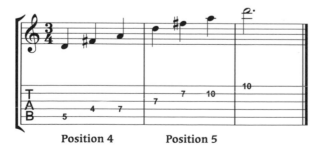

Position 4   Position 5

The 2nd option for playing arpeggios over triads is – as the name already indicates – to do so over three strings. This enables us to play all three notes simultaneously. Figure 34 shows the four options for playing C major triads in root position.

[Figure 34: C Major triads over three strings]

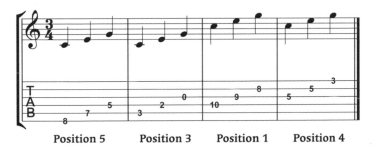

Position 5   **Position 3**   **Position 1**   **Position 4**

In these examples, you can easily see that these notes are arranged in thirds. First, we have the major third, followed by the minor third. Such triads, as well as melodies in which the notes are positioned on neighboring strings, are ideal for techniques like 'Economy Picking' or 'Sweeping'. You move the pick through the strings in one stroke, but make sure the sounds don't blend.

Besides guitarists of jazz and fusion genres, this technique is frequently used by heavy metal guitar players. Don't try to play all five or even six strings at a time to begin with. Take an arpeggio across three strings and try to synchronize the downward progression of your pick with the three notes played one after another. When you master this progression, it is easier to work with more strings. Don't give up, this technique is a huge challenge for most guitarists and it takes time!

Here are some options to combine and link arpeggio fingerings on two or three strings. Here you find an example for position 1 for an A major triad.

[Figure 35: A major triad over 6 strings – position 1]

Position 1 (2 strings) Position 1 (3 strings)

Now find the A major triad in position 5 with the same starting and ending note as in figure 35.

[Figure 36: A major triad over 6 strings – position 5]

Position 5 (3 strings) Position 5 (2 strings)

As you may have noticed, the classification of five positions already pays off. We continue with an E major triad, starting from the A–string in position 4, afterwards from position 3 (figures 37 and 38).

[Figure 37: E major triad over 5 strings – position 4]

Position 4 (2 strings)   Position 4 (3 strings)

[Figure 38: E major triad over 5 strings – position 3]

Position 3 (3 strings)   Position 3 (2 strings)

For the sake of completeness and in order to be able to add intervals later on, here you see position 2 starting from the d–string for the F major triad. In the 2nd measure, you change to position 3.

[Figure 39: F major triad over 4 strings – position 2)]

Position 2 (2 strings)   **Position 3 (2 strings)**

4.2. The Minor Triad

Now it's time for the next chord-type, namely the minor chord. When you flatten the third of a major chord by a semitone, you get a minor chord. It is built from the root, the minor third and the fifth. Here you can see an example of a C minor chord.

Note	Interval	Note	Interval	Note	Chord Type
c	minor third	e♭	major third	g	C minor
Root		Third		Fifth	

Put simply:
Minor third + major third = minor chord.

There are several abbreviations for minor chords. Most commonly, a lower case 'm' is added to the root, for example Cm, Am, Em, and so on. Alternatively the lower case 'm' is replaced by a '–' sign, for example C–, A–, E–, and so on. In classical music and in church hymnbooks, minor chords are often represented by lower case letters, for example c, a, e.

Figure 40, shows the five positions of the C minor arpeggio on the fretboard.

[Figure 40: C minor arpeggio in 5 positions over 2 strings]

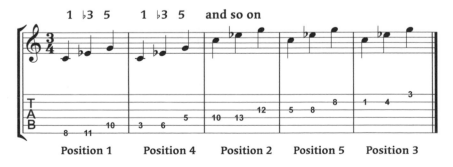

Position 1   **Position 4**   **Position 2**   **Position 5**   **Position 3**

The only difference between the arpeggios of figures 40 and 41 is the position of the minor third, which is now on the next string. You can decide for yourself which of the fingerings you prefer. For horizontal lines, I recommend the fingerings from figure 41. However, you should master both, as you are going to need the fingerings from figure 40 in the chapter about scales and modes (p. 158).

[Figure 41: C minor arpeggio in 5 positions over 2 strings (alternative)]

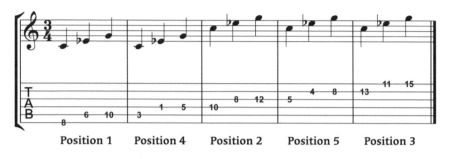

Figure 42, shows the minor arpeggios distributed over three strings, and the layering of a minor third followed by a major third becomes obvious. Due to the number of strings on the guitar, only four positions can be played.

[Figure 42: C minor arpeggios over 3 strings]

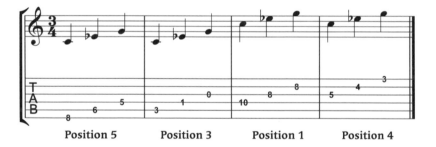

Also, for the minor chords, there are combinations which can be played on more than three strings. Here is an example for A minor in position 1.

[Figure 43: A minor arpeggio – position 1]

34

Of course you can also play the 2nd note (c) on the A–string on the 3rd fret. Try out both versions and decide which fingering you prefer.

When analyzing the solos of your favorite guitarists, you will find out more and more about the material they have used, about the positions they felt at ease with and about those they avoided.

For the A minor arpeggio in position 5 you can perform a finger roll with the little finger, or you can use a slide between the notes a and c' in the 2nd measure and end the finger roll with the index finger.

[Figure 44: A minor arpeggio – position 5]

Position 5 (3 strings) Position 5 (2 strings)

Figures 45 and 46 show the two options we have for D minor arpeggios, starting on the 5th fret on the A–string in positions 4 and 3.

[Figure 45: D minor arpeggio – position 4]

Position 4 (2 strings)   Position 4 (3 strings)

[Figure 46: D minor arpeggio – position 3]

Position 3 (3 strings)   Position 3 (2 strings)

For the sake of completeness, here you see the G minor arpeggio, starting from the d–string in position 2. Again, we change to position 3 in the 2nd bar.

[Figure 47: G minor arpeggio – position 2]

Position 2 (2 strings)   Position 3 (2 strings)

Exercises on minor arpeggios:
Here are exercises for the A minor arpeggio. They are derived from the song Arpeggios from Hell by Yngwie Malmsteen, a Swedish super–shredder on the electric guitar. Malmsteen's neoclassical style often uses arpeggios.

Also practice this line for Cm, Gm, Dm, Fm, Bm, Em, A♭m, F#m, E♭m, B♭m, and C#m.

[Figure 48: Exercise for an arpeggio in A minor]

4.3. The Diminished Triad

Take a minor chord and flatten its fifth by a semitone – the result is a diminished triad. The label for this chord is abbreviated with 'dim' or an '°'.

Note	Interval	Note	Interval	Note	Chord Type
c	minor third	e♭	minor third	g♭	C diminished
Root		Third		dimin. Fifth	

Put simply:
Minor third + minor third = diminished chord.

The diminished fifth is also called a 'tritone'. In seventh chords, which we will treat later on in chapter 9, the tritone is going to gain high significance.

[Figure 49: Arpeggio in C diminished over 2 strings]

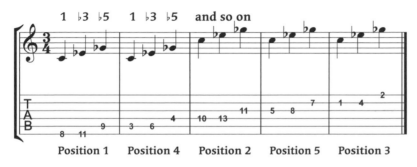

Figure 50, shows the alternative fingerings for the arpeggios over two strings. These alternative fingerings are of help when you explore the fretboard horizontally.

[Figure 50: Arpeggio in C diminished, alternative over 2 strings]

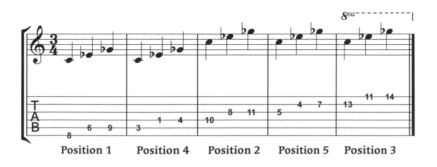

Here you can see arpeggios in C diminished over two strings in the four possible positions.

[Figure 51: Arpeggio in C diminished over 3 strings]

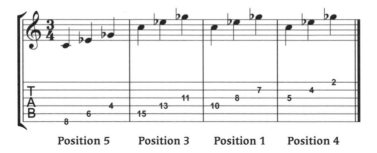

Position 5   Position 3   Position 1   Position 4

In the following figures, you will find the combination of arpeggios over two and three strings in the corresponding positions. First, I will show you position 1.

[Figure 52: Arpeggio in A diminished – position 1]

Position 1 (2 strings)   Position 1 (3 strings)

Figures 53 to 56, show the remaining diminished arpeggios in the corresponding positions as combinations across two or three strings.

[Figure 53: Arpeggio in A diminished – position 5]

Position 5 (3 strings)   Position 5 (2 strings)

[Figure 54: Arpeggio in E diminished – position 4]

Position 4 (2 strings)   Position 4 (3 strings)

[Figure 55: Arpeggio in E diminished – position 3]

Position 3 (3 strings)   Position 3 (2 strings)

In the 2nd bar of figure 56, we change to position 3 again.

[Figure 56: Arpeggio in F diminished – position 2]

Position 2 (2 strings)   Position 3 (2 strings)

4.4. The Augmented Triad

Last but not least, I will show you the triads with two major thirds: the augmented triads, which are abbreviated to 'aug'. In some books, the augmented triad is represented with a '+' instead of '#5', referring to its augmented fifth.

Here is the formula:

Note	Interval	Note	Interval	Note	Chord Type
c	major third	e	major third	g♯	C augmented
Root		Third		augment. Fifth	

Put simply:
Major third + major third = augmented chord.

As the augmented chord is not used very often, I will just give a short overview of these arpeggios. The figures 57 and 58 show arpeggios over two or three strings.

[Figure 57: Arpeggio in C augmented over 2 strings]

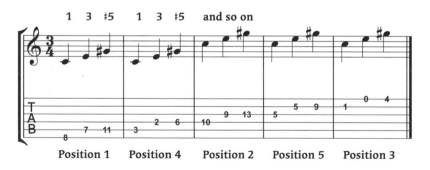

[Figure 58: Arpeggio in C augmented over 3 strings]

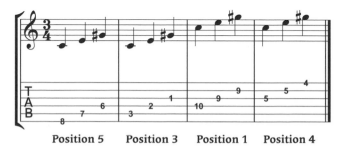

Next, you see the combined augmented arpeggios in the five positions, using two or three strings.

[Figure 59: Arpeggio in G augmented – Position 1]

Position 1 (2 strings) Position 1 (3 strings)

[Figure 60: Arpeggio in A augmented – Position 5]

Position 5 (3 strings)   Position 5 (2 strings)

[Figure 61: D augmented – Position 4]

Position 4 (2 strings)   Position 4 (3 strings)

[Figure 62: D augmented – Position 3]

Position 3 (3 strings)   Position 3 (2 strings)

[Figure 63: E augmented – Position 2]

Position 2 (2 strings)   Position 3 (2 strings)

Exercises on Triads

To help you memorize these four types of triads, practice following exercises. First, in exercises 1–4 (figures 64–67) you find the four different chord types in the five possible positions displayed next to each other. In each one, we begin in position 1 and progress to position 5 step by step. Each of the arpeggios starts with the root.

8-11

[Figure 64: Arpeggio in C major in all 5 positions]

12 - 15

[Figure 65: Arpeggio in C minor in all 5 positions]

[Figure 66: Arpeggio in C diminished in all 5 positions]

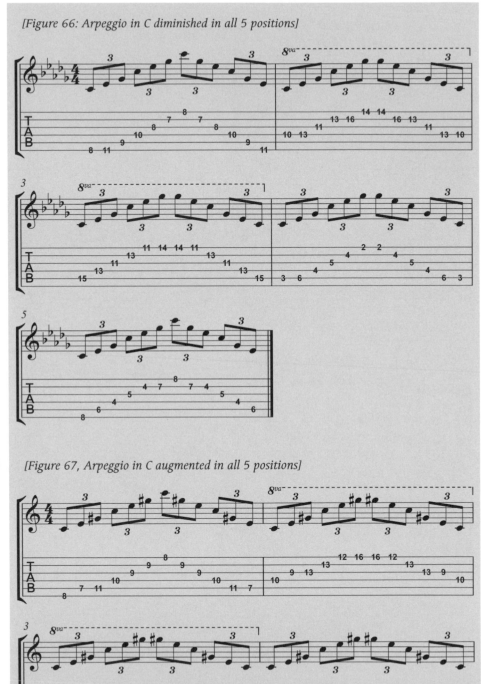

[Figure 67, Arpeggio in C augmented in all 5 positions]

8-23

The next exercise combines keys, chord types and positions. Practice all arpeggios of a chord type in a certain position in every key. Take a look at the Appendix (p. 191) for the chord progressions.

First, practice in a very slow tempo without the playback. Once you master a position, you can start practicing with the playbacks, which have four different levels of difficulty, depending on the tempo.

Here's a short overview to help you find the right tracks for each session.

If you start on level 1 (54 bpm), the order of tracks is:
Track 8 (major) – Track 12 (minor) – Track 16 (diminished) – Track 20 (augmented)
For level 2 (66 bpm), the order of tracks is:
Track 9 (major) – Track 13 (minor) – Track 17 (diminished) – Track 21 (augmented)
For advanced players on level 3 (78 bpm), the order of tracks is:
Track 10 (major) – Track 14 (minor) – Track 18 (diminished) – Track 22 (augmented)
For professionals and aspiring professionals (level 4, 90 bpm), the order of tracks is:
Track 11 (major) – Track 15 (minor) – Track 19 (diminished) – Track 23 (augmented)

Tip: If the tempo steps of the playbacks are too big for you, practice the exercise with a metronome and set the tempo in between the playback tempo indications.

Figure 68 shows this exercise with the major arpeggio in position 1. Proceed as follows:
⇨ Choose a position (1 to 5)

⇨ Practice the major arpeggio in the chosen position (tracks 8–11)

⇨ Practice the minor arpeggio in the chosen position (tracks 12–15)

⇨ Practice the diminished arpeggio in the chosen position (tracks 16–19)

⇨ Practice the augmented arpeggio in the chosen position (tracks 20–23)

Once you have mastered this exercise with position 1 in a certain tempo, go on to the next position and practice it again. You can find the order of chords in the appendix of this book below the corresponding tracks.

As promised, figure 68 shows the exercise on the major arpeggio in position 1.

[Figure 68: The arpeggio in major (position 1) in all keys]

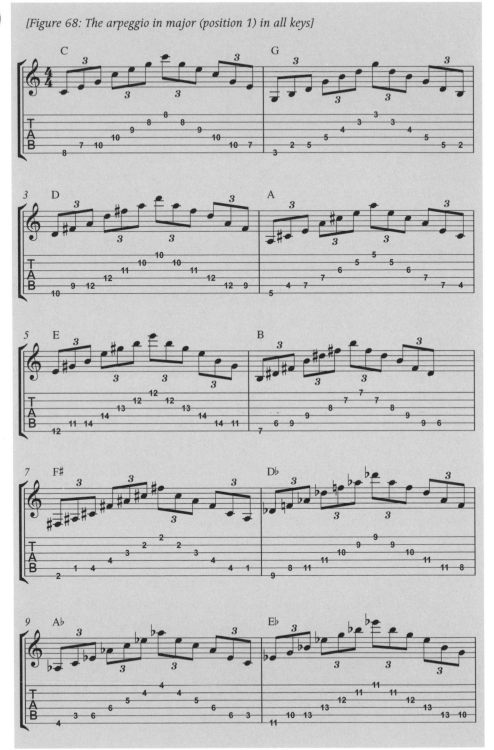

4.5. The Major Keys

Musical flexibility requires the mastering of all keys. In this chapter, you will learn how to build the remaining major keys and discover how they are represented on the fretboard. The system is easy and transparent. Let's declare C major the 'mother' of all major keys from which we can derive everything. If you already know how to work out keys with the help of the circle of fifths and fourths, you are welcome to skip this chapter.

The Circle of Fifths

The circle of fifths represents the so-called #–keys (sharp–side keys), which sharpens (raise) certain notes by a semitone. First, find the 5th note of the scale, which in C major is g. So, g is the root of the new key. The new scale from g looks like this:

g–a–b–c–d–e–f–g'

Now look at the position of the semitone steps in C major: they are between the 3rd/4th and the 6th/7th notes of the scale. But as the 2nd semitone step is supposed to be between the 7th and 8th notes, we need to raise the 7th note of the scale using a #–accidental. F becomes f# (f sharp). Moreover, we get a whole tone step between the 6th and 7th notes. This is why the G–scale requires a #–accidental:

g–a–b–c–d–e– f#–g'

The next scale forms on the 5th note of G major, which is d. The simplest way to find the right notes is as follows:
• Take over existing accidentals into the new key
• The 7th note of the new scale is raised by a semitone.

You can count up to the 7th note of each key, but you will come to the same result if you simply take the penultimate note and raise it by a semitone. In D major, this would be c, raised to c#.

The order of the keys in the circle of fifths is:
G – D – A – E – B – F#

You will have to learn this order by heart.

If you want to know the accidentals of E major, for example, you write down the notes of the C major scale, starting and ending with e:

e   f   g   a   b   c   d   e

In order to fix the accidentals, remember the following:

E major comes fourth in the order. Therefore, we have to place four accidentals.

We can use the following phrase and count four words:

Father Charles Goes Down And Ends Battle

The first letter of each word indicates the note where an accidental has to be placed: f, c, g and d.

So, we get the E major scale:

E   f#   g#   a   b   c#   d#   e

Applying this phrase for other keys, we get:

f# in G major (Father)

f# and c# in D major (Father, Charles)

f#, c#, and g# in A major (Father, Charles, Goes)

… and so on!

In the following figures you will find the six #–keys represented horizontally on the d–string.

[Figure 69: G major]

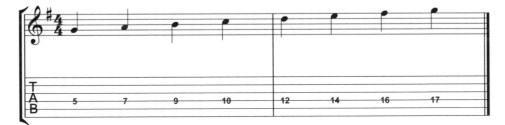

[Figure 70: D major]

[Figure 71: A major]

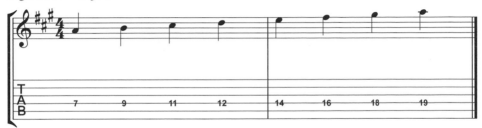

[Figure 72: E major]

[Figure 73: B major]

[Figure 74: F# major]

The Circle of Fourths

The circle of fourths represents the keys with a ♭–accidental, which means keys where some notes need to be flattened. We take the C major scale as a starting point again. The 4th note of the scale is f. Now, let's build the scale from f to f':

f - g - a - b - c - d - e - f'

Here we get semitone steps between the 4th/5th and the 7th/8th notes. But in order to create the required semitone step between the 3rd and the 4th note, the 4th note, b, has to be flattened with a ♭–accidental to b♭. By doing so, we automatically get the required whole tone step between the 4th and the 5th note, and the new scale looks like this:
f–g–a– b♭–c–d–e–f'

Now the 4th note of this new scale, b♭, is the root of the next scale in the order. Similar to the sharp–side keys, the required ♭–accidentals are taken over into the new key and the 4th note of the new key is flattened with an additional ♭–accidental.

The order of the keys in the circle of fourths is:
F – B♭ – E♭ – A♭ – D♭ – G♭.

You will have to learn this order by heart, too.
Let's determine the accidentals of A♭ major, for example:
Write down the notes of the C major scale, beginning and ending with a.
1. The 4th note in F major is b♭, therefore, flatten the note b to b♭.
2. The 4th note in B♭ major is e♭, therefore, flatten the note e to e♭.
3. The 4th note in E♭ major is a♭, therefore, flatten the note a to a♭.
4. The 4th note of A♭ major is d♭, therefore, flatten the note d to d♭.

You've probably noticed, we always flatten the 4th note of the key, and from there we get the next key. So you can already detect the accidental(s) of a key when you have a look at the first letter of the key that follows. For example, F major gets one b♭, as you can see on the starting letter of the next key in the order: B♭. Accordingly, B♭ major gets accidentals for the notes b (battle) and e (ends): b♭ and e♭.

You can also memorize the order of the ♭-accidentals by citing the phrase for the #-accidentals backwards:

Battle Ends And Down Goes Charles' Father.

In the 1st key (F major), we get b♭.
In the 2nd key (B♭ major), we get b♭ and e♭.
In the 3rd key (E♭ major), we get b♭, e♭, and a♭.
In the 4th key (A♭ major), we get b♭, e♭, a♭ and d♭.
… and so on!

In the following figures, you will see all keys of the circle of fourths played on the d–string. D♭ major starts on the d–string on the 11th fret and reaches up to the 23th fret. So this key cannot be played horizontally on the d–string on conventional electric guitars equipped with 21 or 22 frets.

[Figure 75: F major]

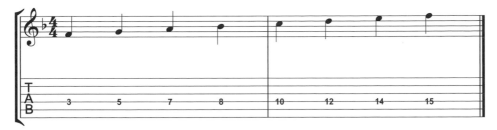

[Figure 76: B♭ major]

[Figure 77: E♭ major]

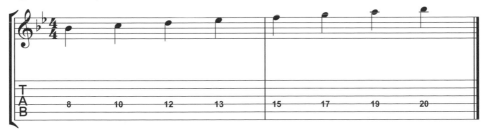

[Figure 78: A♭ major]

[Figure 79: D♭ major]

[Figure 80: Gb major]

Scales which contain basically the same notes but have different accidentals (for example F# major and Gb major) are described by the term 'enharmonic equivalent'.

4.6. The Diatonic Triads

Diatonic means that all notes have to be part of a certain scale and no other notes must be used. Let's have a look at the diatonic triads within the major scale by harmonizing the individual notes. The C major scale will again serve as an example. We label the steps of the scale using Roman numerals.

Step	Root	Third	Fifth	Chord type
I.	c	e	g	C Major
II.	d	f	a	D Minor
III.	e	g	b	E Minor
IV.	f	a	c	F Major
V.	g	b	d	G Major
VI.	a	c	e	A Minor
VII.	b	d	f	B Diminished

■ **Note:** In each major key, we have major chords on the degrees I, IV, and V. On the steps II, III, and VI, we have minor chords, and a diminished chord on step VII.

Exercises on the diatonic triads

Here are five exercises, below, which help to transfer the diatonic triads to the fretboard and to your ear. You will find rhythmic variations of these patterns in the solos of many of your heroes.

Exercise 1

Exercise 1 demonstrates how the diatonic triads of C major are distributed over two strings. We take the note c on the A–string on the 3rd fret as a starting note.

[Figure 81: The diatonic triads of C major over 2 strings]

Practice the diatonic triads over two strings in the keys given below. The starting notes of each key are shown in brackets:

G Major (E–string 3rd fret, d–string 5th fret)
D Major (A–string 5th fret, b–string 3rd fret)
A Major (g–string 2nd fret, E–string 5th fret)
E Major (d–string 2nd fret, b–string 5th fret)
B Major (A–string 2nd fret, g–string 4th fret)
F Major (E–string 1st fret, d–string 3rd fret, b–string 6th fret)

Then play the exercises backwards!

Exercise 2

Exercise 2 demonstrates how the diatonic triads are distributed on three strings.

[Figure 82: The diatonic triads of C major over 3 strings]

Practice the diatonic triads over three strings in the following keys. The starting notes of each key are shown in brackets:

G Major (E–string 3rd fret, d–string 5th fret)
D Major (A–string 5th fret, g–string 7th fret)
A Major (g–string 2nd fret, E–string 5th fret)
E Major (d–string 2nd fret, A–string 7th fret)
B Major (g–string 4th fret, E–string 7th fret)
F Major (d–string 3rd fret, A–string 8th fret)

Then play the exercises backwards!

Exercise 3

Next, three exercises with arpeggios. Exercise 3 (figure 83) shows a D major arpeggio in triplets over two octaves in position 3. You might use the sweeping–technique.

[Figure 83: Arpeggio in D major over 2 octaves in 8ᵗʰ note triplets]

Also play this exercise with the arpeggios spanning two octaves in positions 1, 4, and 5, and vary the chord type (major, minor, diminished, and augmented).

Then, apply the exercise to the diatonic triads of the following keys. The individual shapes of the diatonic degrees remain the same; you only shift the root. Be careful to use the correct chord types within each key!

D Major (Position 3, A–string 5ᵗʰ fret)
G Major (Position 1, E–string 3ʳᵈ fret)
C Major (Position 4, A–string 3ʳᵈ fret)
A Major (Position 5, E–string 5ᵗʰ fret)

Exercise 4

This exercise creates an interesting sound, as the 16th notes are phrased in groups of three. Use the metronome in order to avoid tripping back into a triplet pattern!

[Figure 84: Arpeggio in E minor spanning two octaves in a 3 against 4 pattern]

Also play this exercise with the arpeggios spanning two octaves in positions 1, 4 and 5, and vary the chord type (major, minor, diminished, and augmented).

Now play the exercise over the diatonic triads of the keys given below. The individual shapes of the diatonic degrees remain the same; you only shift the root. Be careful to use the correct chord types within each key!

D Major (Position 3, A–string 5th fret)
G Major (Position 1, E–string 3rd fret)
C Major (Position 4, A–string 3rd fret)
A Major (Position 5, E–string 5th fret)

Exercise 5

Exercise 5 (figure 85) shows the diatonic triads of D major in 16th-notes triplets. Here, your pattern is: down–down–down–down–down–up–down–up–up–up–up–up, and so on.

Also play this exercise in 8th notes, 8th note triplets and 16th notes. By varying the note length you can adjust sweeping arpeggios to the tempo of the song into which you might want to insert them. If the song is very fast, use 8th notes or 8th note triplets; you can try 16th notes or 16th note triplets in slow tempos.

Now play the exercise over the diatonic triads of the following keys. The individual shapes of the diatonic degrees remain the same; you only shift the root. Be careful to use the correct chord types within each key!

D Major (Position 3, A–string 5th fret)
G Major (Position 1, E–string 3rd fret)
C Major (Position 4, A–string 3rd fret)
A Major (Position 5, E–string 5th fret)

[Figure 85: Ascending diatonic triads in D major, 16th notes triplets]

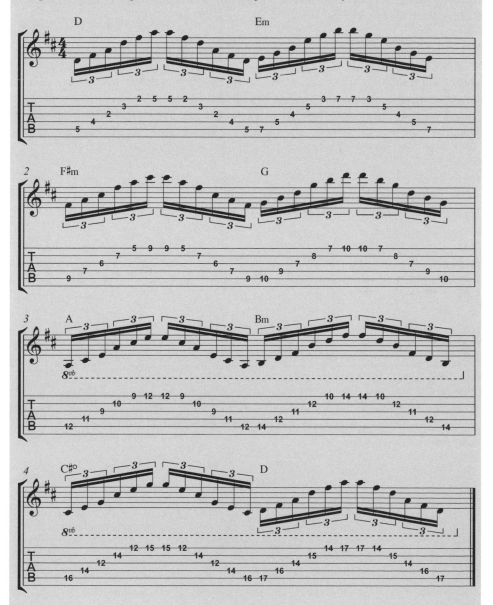

4.7. The Classic Cadence

The Major Cadence

The three major chords of the major scale form the main chords of a key. The major chord on the 1st degree (I) is called the tonic, the chord on the 4th degree (IV) is the subdominant, and the chord on the 5th degree (V) is known as the dominant. The chord on the 5th degree is mostly played as a dominant seventh chord, the structure of which I will present in the chapter about seventh chords.

The 'classic' cadence consists of the sequence of these chords: I–IV–V–I.

Using the example of C major, this would be the sequence of the chords C–F–G–C. Due to the upward progression of a whole tone step, the subdominant F leads to the dominant G. During the progression from the dominant G to the tonic C, the third of the dominant resolves into the root of C. Due to its striving for the root c, the b of our example is called guide note. Generally, the guide note is the seventh note of a scale.

In the following example, this cadence is shown in classic notation. The key is C major.

[Figure 86: The classic cadence in major]

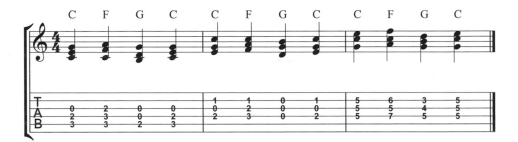

When you play these examples, you hear how conclusive this cadence sounds. You might notice that you have probably played and heard it many times before, whether consciously or unconsciously.

Exercises on the classic major cadence

Exercise 1

The following applies to all exercises with arpeggios and cadences: You should determine the arpeggios of the triads via their positions within a fretboard area.

In figure 87, you will see the sequence of the arpeggios of the classic cadence, using the example of G major. So, G is the tonic, C is the subdominant, and D is the dominant.

The sequence is:

Tonic G major (position 1) – subdominant C (position 4) – dominant D (position 3)
Tonic G major (position 2) – subdominant C (position 5) – dominant D (position 4)
Tonic G major (position 3) – subdominant C (position 1) – dominant D (position 5)
Tonic G major (position 4) – subdominant C (position 2) – dominant D (position 1)
Tonic G major (position 5) – subdominant C (position 3) – dominant D (position 2)

[Figure 87: Exercise on cadences in major in all 5 positions: G major]

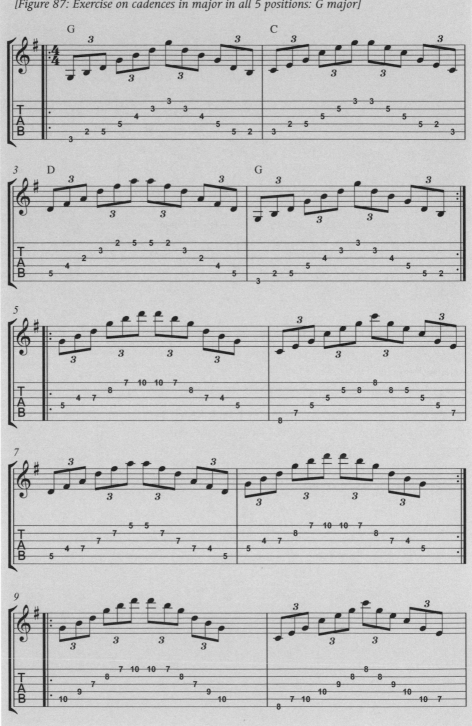

⇨ Determine a fretboard area for the cadence, for example tonic C in position 1.

⇨ Play the cadence of C major in this fretboard area and repeat it.

⇨ Take the position of the tonic, change to the next key of the circle of fifths and play the corresponding cadence.

⇨ Practice this for all # keys.

⇨ Go back to C major and play it once more.

⇨ Take the position of the tonic, change to the next key of the circle of fourths and play the corresponding cadence.

⇨ Practice the cadence for all ♭ keys, too.

Now, determine a new fretboard area, for example, tonic C in position 2. Practice the cadence in this fretboard area, starting at step two of this exercise.

24-25

Exercise 2 [CD 24-25]
For this exercise, you might want to use tracks 24 (circle of fifths) and 25 (circle of fourths) of the playback CD. The chord progression is as follows:

I – I – IV – IV – V – V – I – I – IV – V – I – I

⇨ You will find the chords in the appendix for the corresponding tracks.

⇨ Determine a fretboard area, for example tonic C in position 1.

⇨ Play along the chord progression with the arpeggios in this fretboard area (track 24).

⇨ Maintain the position of the tonic and shift it to the next key.

⇨ Repeat this procedure during the whole track.

⇨ Then, practice the cadences of the circle of fourths with the same starting position as you applied to C major (track 25).

Define a new fretboard area for the tonic, for example, tonic C in position 2 and start again at step 2 of this exercise.

The Minor Cadence

The 'natural' minor scale is built on the 6th (VI) degree of the major scale . This scale is also known as the relative minor key to a certain major key. In C major, this would be the natural A minor scale.

[Figure 88: The natural A minor scale]

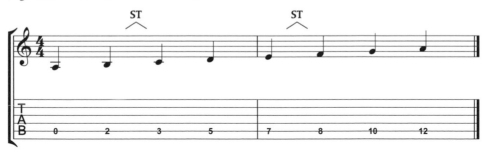

The semitones in the natural minor scale are between the 2nd/3rd and the 5th/6th note. If we build the minor cadence in the same way as the major cadence, we get A minor as our tonic and d minor as the subdominant. The dominant can be found via an additional step: as you know from the previous chapters, the third of the dominant (guide note) resolves (a semitone step upwards) into the root of the tonic. However, in our example, the triad on the 5th degree (V) is an E minor chord with the third g. Therefore, it takes two semitones to reach the root a. Now, sharpen the g to a g# and you get an E major chord instead of a minor chord. A new scale arises, which is called the 'harmonic' minor. You will find more information on this topic in chapter 12.1.

[Figure 89: The harmonic minor scale in A]

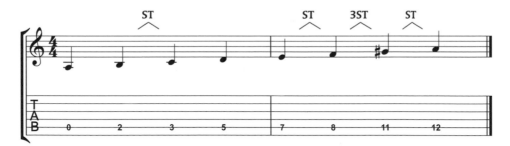

For the cadence in A minor, we use the chords Am as the tonic, Dm as the subdominant, and E major as the dominant.

[Figure 90: Cadence in A minor]

Exercises on the minor cadence

Exercise 1

First, prepare the connecting positions of the triads within a fretboard area. Here we see the example of the cadence of Am – Dm – E – Am.

Tonic Am position 1 – subdominant Dm position 4 – dominant E position 3
Tonic Am position 2 – subdominant Dm position 5 – dominant E position 4
Tonic Am position 3 – subdominant Dm position 1 – dominant E position 5
Tonic Am position 4 – subdominant Dm position 2 – dominant E position 1
Tonic Am position 5 – subdominant Dm position 3 – dominant E position 2

In figure 91 on page 64 you will find the cadence in complete notation for all five positions.

Determine a fretboard area for the cadence, for example, tonic Am in position 1. Play the cadence Am – Dm – E – Am.

Maintain the determined position of the tonic and play the following cadences:

Em – Am – B – Em
Bm – Em – F# – Bm
F#m – Bm – C# – F#m
C#m – F#m – G# – C#m
G#m – C#m – D# – G#m
Ebm – Abm – Bb – Ebm
Bbm – Ebm – F – Bbm
Fm – Bbm – C – Fm
Cm – Fm – G – Cm
Gm – Cm – D – Gm
Dm – Gm – A – Dm

Determine the next fretboard area for the tonic, for example, position 2, and start again.

Exercise 2

For this exercise, you need tracks 26 (circle of fifths) and 27 (circle of fourths) of the playback CD. The chord progression is as follows:

26-27

Im – Im – IVm – IVm – V – V – Im – Im – IVm – V – Im – Im

⇨ You will find the chords in the appendix with their corresponding tracks.

⇨ Determine a fretboard area, for example, tonic Am in position 1.

⇨ Play the chord progression with the arpeggios in this fretboard area (track 26).

⇨ Maintain the position of the tonic and shift it to the next key.

⇨ Proceed like this throughout the whole track.

⇨ Practice the cadences in the circle of fourths with the same starting position as A minor (track 27).

Define a new fretboard area for the tonic, for example, tonic Am in position 2, and start again at step 2.

[Figure 91: The cadence of A minor in all 5 positions]

66

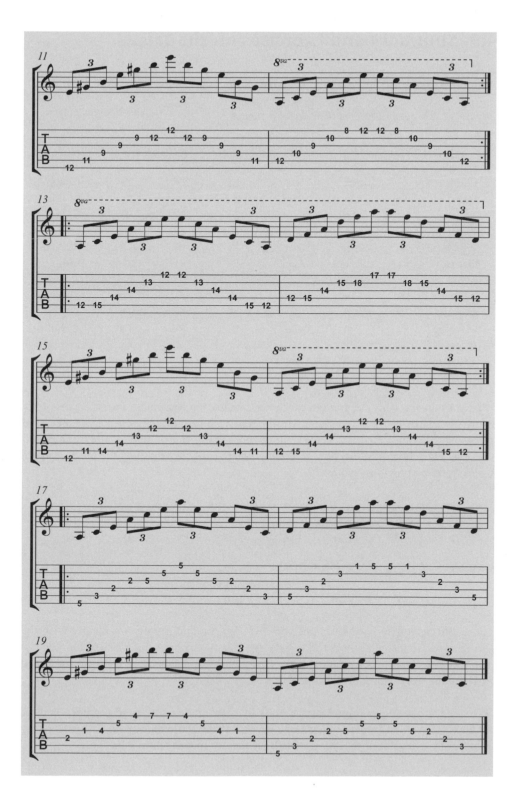

4.9. Summary and Exercises on the Triads

In figure 92, you will find a tabular overview of the major keys.

[Figure 92: The major keys and their diatonic chords]

Key	I. Degree	II. Degree	III. Degree	IV. Degree	V. Degree	VI. Degree	VII. Degree
C major	C	Dm	Em	F	G	Am	B dim
G major	G	Am	Bm	C	D	Em	F♯ dim
D major	D	Em	F♯m	G	A	Bm	C♯ dim
A major	A	Bm	C♯m	D	E	F♯m	G♯ dim
E major	E	F♯m	G♯m	A	B	C♯m	D♯ dim
B major	B	C♯m	D♯m	E	F♯	G♯m	A♯ dim
F♯ major	F♯	G♯m	A♯m	B	C♯	D♯m	E♯ dim
G♭ major	G♭	A♭m	B♭m	C♭	D♭	E♭m	F dim
D♭ major	D♭	E♭m	Fm	G♭	A♭	B♭m	C dim
A♭ major	A♭	B♭m	Cm	D♭	E♭	Fm	G dim
E♭ major	E♭	Fm	Gm	A♭	B♭	Cm	D dim
B♭ major	B♭	Cm	Dm	E♭	F	Gm	A dim
F major	F	Gm	Am	B♭	C	Dm	E dim

With the table in figure 92, you can check out, practice, and transpose the arpeggios nicely using the 'Nashville' notation system. In the Nashville system, only the step of the chord to be played is indicated. Thus, each chord progression can be immediately transposed into every key. However, this system requires you to really master the principle of diatonic scales from the previous chapter.

Let's take a key, for example, G major, and note down a chord progression:

G	D	Em	C	Am	C	D	G

– expressed in steps, it looks like this:

I	V	VIm	IV	IIm	IV	V	I

Try recording yourself at home; this will give you the opportunity to practice with the recordings. Of course, it's more fun to have another guitarist as a duo partner. But you can also take your favorite songs and practice along with the playback. In this case, you need to know the song's key and chord progression.

Have a go at creating an improvisation on triads! Note down any chord progressions you might want to try and practice them in all keys using the Nashville system. The easiest way is to mostly use notes of the chords' triads, as they fit into the harmonies best.

In figure 93, you will find ten examples which might serve as an inspiration for your improvisations. First, concentrate on a rhythmic pattern and practice it with your chord progressions. Once you have done this in all keys, try the next pattern.

On the CD you will find playbacks (tracks 28–30). Track 28 is in the funk style with one-bar chord changes, and track 29 contains a reggae with two–bar changes. Track 30 is a bossa nova with two–bar changes.

You will find the corresponding chord progressions in the appendix.

[Figure 93: Rehearsal pattern for triads]

28-30

Here is an exercise in F major with melody pattern 2.

28

[Figure 94: Melody pattern 2 in F major / D minor chord progressions]

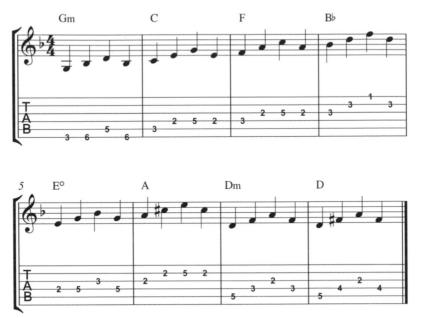

As it becomes clear, the fretboard area can stay the same throughout the exercise.

Before each exercise, think about the positions of the triads on the fretboard area that you would like to practice. The best way is to note it down in advance. Also try to mix the variants of two and three strings. For the exercise in figure 94, this could be:

Gm in position 1 over two strings
C in position 4 over two strings
F in position 2 over two strings
B♭ in position 4 over three strings
Edim in position 2 over two strings
A in position 5 over two strings
Dm in position 3 over three strings
D in position 3 over three strings

CHAPTER 5 Triads and their Inversions

In this chapter I will show you the remaining options for playing a triad. For this we need to understand the term 'voicing': Voicing describes the order of notes in a chord.

Triads contain, as the name indicates, three different notes. In the exercises on arpeggios we structured them in thirds. The lowest note was the root, the third took up the mid-position, and the fifth represented the top note. This structure is called the root position. In C major, we have the order c–e–g.

Now, take the lowest note c and play it one octave higher: e–g–c'. The result is still a C major chord, but it has left its root position and changed into the 1st inversion. Next, take the note e (the third of the chord) and play it one octave higher. The resulting order is g–c'–e'. This voicing is called 2nd inversion. When you play the note g one octave higher, you will get the root position again, but transposed by an octave.

Therefore, there are three options for building voicings of triads:

Root position (RP)	Root	Third	Fifth
1st inversion	Third	Fifth	Root
2nd inversion	Fifth	Root	Third

The following figure shows the three voicings of a C major chord on the strings a, d, and g.

[Figure 95: The 3 voicings of a C major chord]

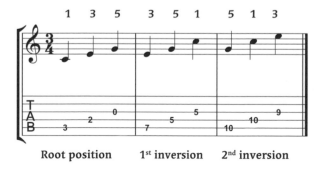

        Root position   **1st inversion**   **2nd inversion**

In the following figures you will see minor, diminished, and augmented chords in root position and in their two inversions, following the same system. Figure 97 shows the diminished chords with the root d, as the diminished 5th of the root c cannot be represented on this fretboard area.

[Figure 96: The 3 voicings of a Cm chord]

Root position   1ˢᵗ inversion   2ⁿᵈ inversion

[Figure 97: The 3 voicings of a Ddim chord]

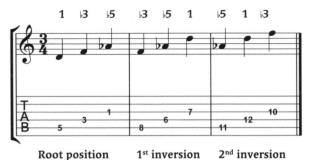

Root position   1ˢᵗ inversion   2ⁿᵈ inversion

[Figure 98: The 3 voicings of a Caug chord]

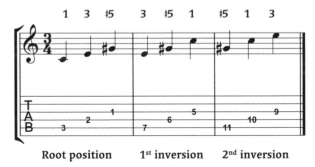

Root position   1ˢᵗ inversion   2ⁿᵈ inversion

How can we use chords and their inversions? First, we can create a logical and coherent melody part within a chord progression. Secondly, each voicing has got a characteristic sound. So, if the root position appears to sound too boring or unimaginative, try out the inversions of the chord. The modified interval structure might inspire you.

Now, explore the new sound possibilities of the voicings and areas for their application. First, I'll show you the chords where the notes are distributed on the strings g, b, and e'. These voicings are ideal for creating a funky sound, or can be used as an alternative for a 2ⁿᵈ guitar part.

[Figure 99: Triads in root position on the strings g–b–e']

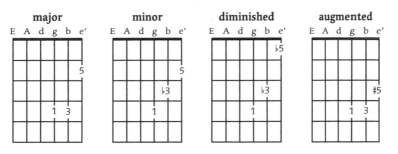

Here you see the chord diagrams of the root positions of the four chord types. The numbers represent the functions of the notes within the chords. I've not given any fingerings, as they can vary depending on the preceding chord and the direction in which you are heading. It's more important for you to learn the interval positions on the strings.

If you have already mastered the formation of triads, it might be enough to know the major forms; you can easily build the minor forms by flattening the third. The chord diagrams do not prescribe a certain note or fret; with your knowledge about the notes on the different strings you can choose your own system.

For the chords in figure 99, the root lies on the g–string. If you are a visual type of a learner, just study the chord diagrams. As the figures are positioned directly next to each other, the minimal changes are easier to notice and to 'store'.

> **Tip:** It's enough to know one fingering for augmented chords for each string trio. As this chord type is entirely built of major thirds, the inversions look identical.

Figure 100 shows the 1st inversion of the triads on the high strings. The lowest note lies on the g–string again and forms the third of the corresponding chord. It is easier to learn the position of the root in the chord diagrams than to think 'beyond the third'. You will reach your goal faster.

[Figure 100: Triads in the 1st inversion on the strings g –b– e']

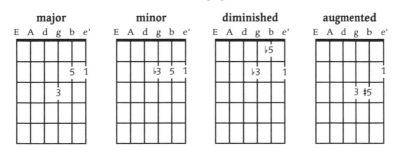

I have not promised too much concerning the augmented chord. It is identical to the fingering of the root position and only differs in the pattern of the chord notes. The same is true for all other augmented chords, the fingering of which stays the same with a spacing of four frets in both ways.

Figure 101 concludes the representation of triads on the three high strings in 2nd inversion.

[Figure 101: Triads on the strings g–b–e' in 2nd inversion]

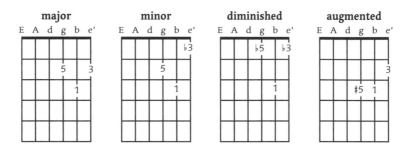

Exercise
The following exercise might help you to optimize your voicing within a chord progression. The corresponding tracks are identical to tracks 28–30, but do not contain rhythm guitar. Figure 102 shows a chord progression in C major.

31-33

[Figure 102: Exercise on voicings: RP = Root Position – 1.Iv = 1st Inversion – 2nd Iv = 2. Inversion]

Chords	Dm	G	C	F	B dim	E	Am	A
Step	IIm	V	I	IV	VII dim	III	VIm	VI
Voicing 1	RP	2. Iv	1. Iv	RP	1. Iv	RP	2. Iv	2. Iv
Voicing 2	1. Iv	RP	2. Iv	1. Iv	2. Iv	1. Iv	RP	RP
Voicing 3	2. Iv	1. Iv	RP	2. Iv	RP	2. Iv	1. Iv	1. Iv

In C major we expect a minor chord on the degrees III and VI. The major chords take on the function of secondary dominants and make the chord progression sound more interesting.
Each of the playbacks is recorded in a different key (see appendix). However, the order of the degrees is the same. Here you can prove that you have understood the Nashville system. You will find the corresponding chord progressions in the appendix.
Let's have a look at the exercise:
⮑ Start with the root position of the first chord, Dm. The root lies on the g–string on the 7th fret.

⮑ Determine the root of the next chord, G major, in this fretboard area on the strings g–b–e'. It lies on the b–string on the 8th fret. Play the chord with the fingering of the 2nd inversion. When changing from Dm to G major, the note on the g–string remains, whereas the notes on the b– and e'– strings shift two semitones upwards.

⮑ Determine the root of the chord, C, in this fretboard area. It lies on the e'–string on the 8th fret. Thus, play C with the fingering of the 1st inversion. When changing from G to C, the middle voice remains (b–string, 8th fret). The remaining voices shift upwards: the bass voice moves two semitones higher, and the melody one.

⇨ Determine the root of the chord F in this fretboard area. It lies on the g–string on the 10th fret. Thus, play F in root position. When changing from C to F, the melody part remains, whereas the bass and middle voices move upwards one or two semitones, respectively.

⇨ Repeat this procedure for the rest of the chord progression.

Of course, the individual voicings do not have to move upwards; try a downward voicing too. Most times, the chord progressions are very consistent, which means that one or two notes of the preceding chord can remain. The exception is the shift from the subdominant to the dominant, where you can simply shift the chord two semitones upwards (or downwards, respectively).

[Figure 103: The roots of the exercise on chords]

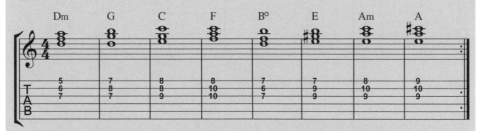

31-33

[Figure 104: Complete voicings for the exercise on chords]

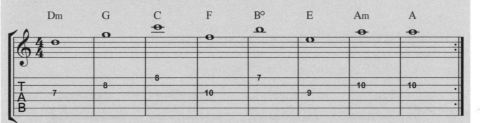

31-33

⇨ Now, play the first chord, Dm, in the 1st inversion. From this fingering, you can derive the 2nd chord in root position, the 3rd chord in the 2nd inversion, and so on.

⇨ Now, play the first chord, Dm, in the 2nd inversion, G in the 1st inversion, C in root position, and so on.

You are probably going to hate this exercise the first few times you practice it, but if you stay on the ball, you will make huge progress in mastering the fretboard. Your own sound spectrum is going to expand, because the notes of the chords can interlock, just like on a piano.

In the next step, we'll practice the voicings on the strings d, g, and b. These voicings made their appearance particularly in the rock songs of the 80s and 90s. It sounds great when we combine riffs on the A–string with the voicings from A major. A good example is Randy Rhoads' riff in the song Crazy Train by Ozzy Osbourne. Also, Eddie Van Halen and other famous rock guitarists make use of this technique in their music.

[Figure 105: Ozzy Osbourne: Crazy Train]

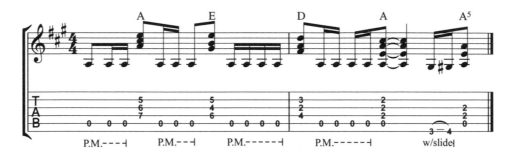

Let's start with the chords in root position.

[Figure 106: Triads in root position on the strings d–g–b]

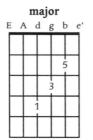

[Figure 107: 1ˢᵗ inversion of triads on the strings d–g–b]

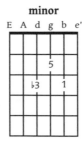
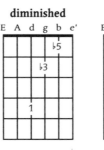

[Figure 108: 2nd inversion of triads in the strings d–g–b]

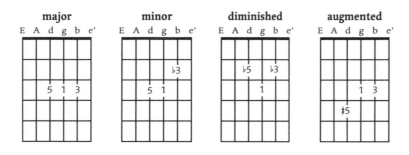

In figures 109–111, I have noted down an 80s style rock riff. The chords of A major, D major, and E major run over the steady, palm muted 8th note bass A. For the three chords, I have used voicings which fit together nicely in terms of their positions. Try to experiment with ideas like these. For example, if your riff is supposed to sound lower, try playing E major chords and use the open E-string for the bass notes. In a drop–D tuning, play the chords of D major. Try playing minor chords in this style, too.

[Figure 109: Rock riff 1, A major]

1

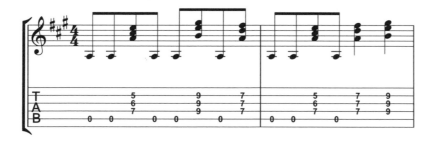

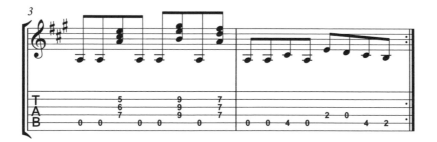

[Figure 110: Rock riff 2, A major]

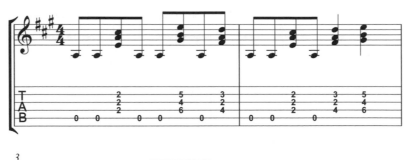

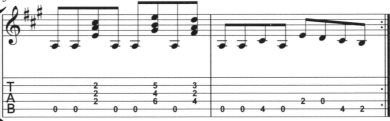

[Figure 111: Rock riff 3, A major]

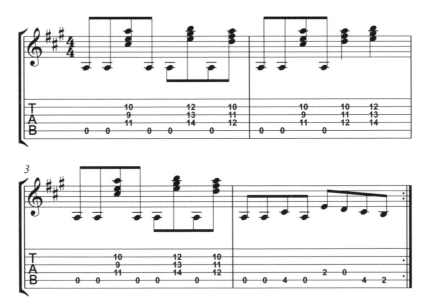

Of course, you can also play the exercise on the voicings in figure 102 with the fingerings of the d–g–b voicings. Furthermore, you can compile sweep picking studies using these voicings. There are many possibilities to choose from. By experimenting, you might find you have an 'eureka' moment. We as guitarists are often 'painting by numbers', that is, we use tablature without even thinking about what we are playing and how we could use it for our own music.

For Heavy Metal fans, we are going to dig deeper. Here, I am going to show you the voicings of the string combinations A–d–g. These can be combined easily with the open E-string.

[Figure 112: Triads in root position on the strings A–d–g]

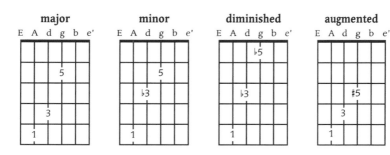

[Figure 113: Triads in 1ˢᵗ inversion on the strings A–d–g]

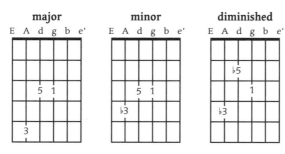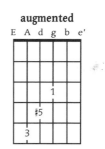

[Figure 114: Triads in 2ⁿᵈ inversion on the strings A–d–g]

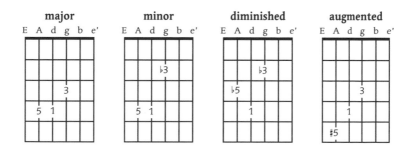

On these three strings, the timbre of the voicing becomes quite dark. As the two higher strings are missing, brilliance and differentiation of the chords get lost easily.

In order to complete our chapter on triads and voicings, I'll present the voicings on the strings E, A, and d. For conventional chord strumming, the presence of the melody strings is clearly missing. However, for picking patterns, it is possible to use such voicings as they offer different sounds while maintaining their timbre. In topics like harmony, composition, melody, and solo structures, you are always going to come across the elementary issue of triads and voicings. The more you know about them and are able to reproduce them, the more versatile and secure your playing is going to be.

[Figure 115: Triads in root position on the strings E–A–d]

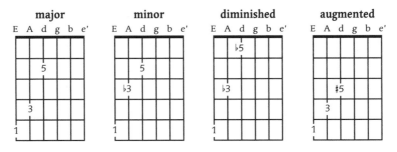

[Figure 116: Triads in 1ˢᵗ inversion on the strings E–A–d]

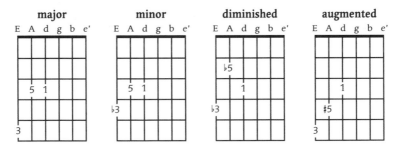

[Figure 117: Triads in 2ⁿᵈ inversion on the strings E–A–d]

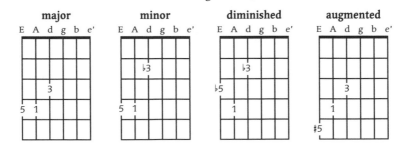

CHAPTER 6 Seconds and Fourths

We have now covered roots, thirds, fifths, chords, voicings and arpeggios. Now it is time to get to know some new intervals. Let's start with the second, which lies between the root and the third. Just like the thirds, seconds are not perfect intervals, but exist as minor (one semitone step) and major (two semitone steps) seconds. The seconds are often used as additions (optional notes) in chords. Then, they get the abbreviation 9 (major second) or ♭9 (minor second). With this numeral, we express that the second is added to the octave of the root. In so-called 'sus chords', we use the abbreviation '2',but we'll learn about that later.

In figure 118 you see the position of the major second in relation to the root c.

[Figure 118: Major second between d and the root c]

The major second can also be played on the next string (see figure 119):

[Figure 119: Major second between d and the root c over 2 strings]

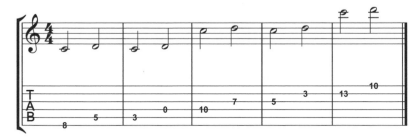

■ **Note:** You can find the major seconds two frets above the root. When the roots are on the E–, A–, d–, or b–string, you can play the major seconds three frets lower on the next higher string (x–3).
If the root lies on the g–string, the major second lies two frets lower on the b–string (x–2).

[Figure 120: The position of the major seconds (2) on the fretboard]

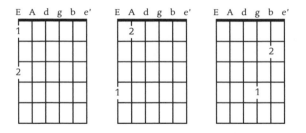

Figure 121 shows the position of the minor second d♭ in relation to c.

[Figure 121: Minor second between c and d♭]

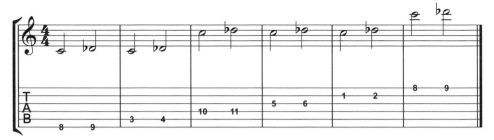

■ **Note:** You can find the minor seconds one fret above the root (x+1). When the root lies on the E–, A–, d–, or b– string, you can also play the minor second four frets lower on the next string (x–4).

If the root lies on the g–string, you can find the minor second on the b–string 3 frets lower (x–3).

[Figure 122: The position of the minor seconds (♭2) on the fretboard]

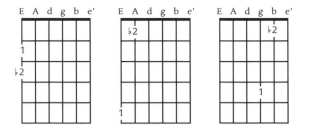

Just like the fifth, the fourth is part of the group of perfect intervals. The distance between the root and its fourth is five semitones. As you know, the guitar is tuned in ascending fourths, with the exception of a major third between g and b. The fourth sounds a little sharper and more distinctive than the fifth. The abbreviation of the fourth is the numeral '4'. In extended chords, the interval abbreviation '11' is used instead of 4.

[Figure 123: The position of the perfect fourth f in relation to the root c]

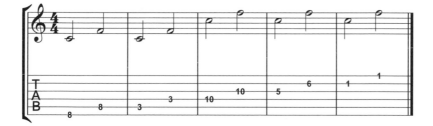

■ **Note:** You can find the fourth on the next higher string on the same fret (x=x). If the root lies on the g–string, you find its fourth on the next fret (x+1) on the b–string.

The fourth is not used in its diminished form, as the resulting four semitone steps are reserved for the major thirds. However, when we want to form the fourth on f in C major, we get the note b, which is six semitone steps away. This interval is called the augmented fourth (in interval notation: #4/#11). Of course, the diminished fifth also has six semitone steps. Despite this, the augmented fourth has to be used in functions different to those of the diminished fifth. You will learn more about this in chapter 11.

[Figure 124: The augmented fourth f# in relation to the root c]

■ **Note:** When the root lies on the E–, A–, d–, or b– string, you find the augmented fourth one fret higher on the next string (x+1). If the root lies on the g–string, you find the augmented fourth two frets higher on the b–string (x+2).

Figure 125 shows the position of the fourths and augmented fourths on the fretboard.

[Figure 125: Position of the fourths (4) and the augmented fourths (#4) on the fretboard]

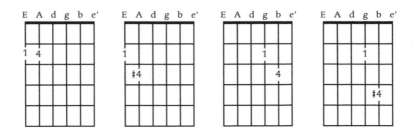

Let's proceed to the chords built of seconds and fourths. When you integrate seconds and fourths into chords, you get so–called 'sus chords'. 'Sus2' is the abbreviation of 'suspended', which describes how the third of the major or minor triad is substituted by the second (2). In a sus4 chord, the third is substituted by the fourth (4). The sus4 chord can frequently be found in classical music, where it is called the 'suspended' fourth. Mostly, these suspensions are resolved downwards to the major third.
In pop and rock music, many songs can be found which profit from the open sound these sus-chords create, for example the keyboard melody of Bryan Adams' Summer of '69, Kansas' Dust in the Wind, and Barclay James Harvest's Hymn.

The chord progression Major – sus4 – Major is often used and has a very characteristic sound. The sus-chords cannot be described in terms of gender, as their sound does not allow conclusions on the chord quality (major or minor). Sus–chords have an open, pending sound and create a great spherical effect.

Try out the effects of the sus-chords by modifying the conventional major or minor chords to sus-chords, and vice versa.

The next figures show sus2 and sus4 chords in connection with the individual voicings of the major and minor chords.

Tip: It can sound great if you exchange minor chords for sus2 chords and major chords for sus4 chords. However, this is not a rule. Anything that sounds good is allowed.

[Figure 126: Major/Minor chords and sus – voicings in root position on the strings g–b–e']

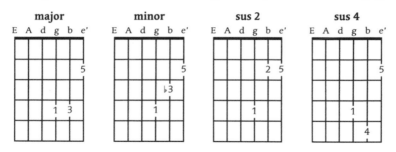

[Figure 127: Major/Minor chords and sus – voicings in 1st inversion on the strings g–b–e']

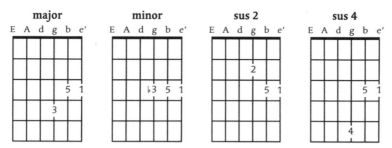

[Figure 128: Major/Minor chords and sus – voicings in 2nd inversion on the strings g–b–e']

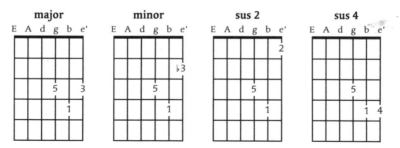

Take the plunge and integrate these sus-chords into your playing, even though they might not be demanded explicitly. Your chord playing will get more melodious and richer. As an example, here is the keyboard–theme from Summer of '69 by Bryan Adams, arranged for guitar.

[Figure 129: Bryan Adams: Summer of 69]

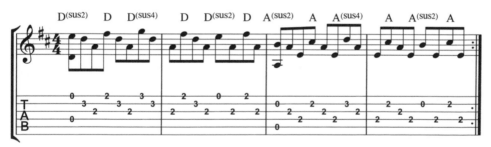

The following figures show the sus chords on the strings d, g, and b. I have noted down some examples for their use.

[Figure 130: Major, minor, and sus – voicings in root position on the strings d, g, b]

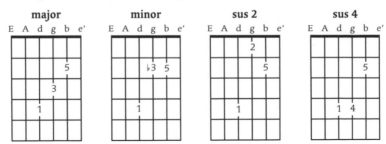

Figure 131 shows a riff with sus2 chords and their resolution into A major.

[Figure 131: Rock riff with Asus4 – A – progression]

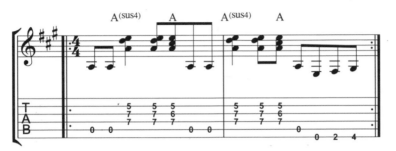

[Figure 132: Major, minor, and sus – voicings in 1ˢᵗ inversion on the strings d, g, b]

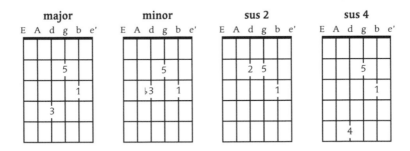

Next example is a picking pattern with sus voicings in A major and E major. Create similar picking patterns or think of a strumming pattern yourself.

[Figure 133: Picking with sus chords]

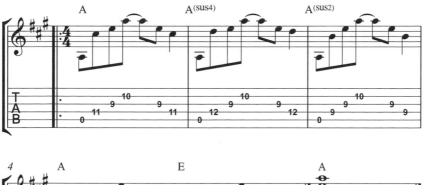

[Figure 134: Major, minor, and sus – voicings in 2nd inversion on the strings d, g, b]

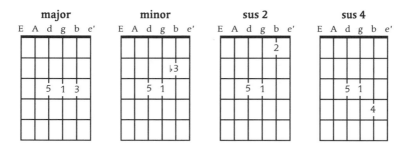

Figure 135 shows a riff in C major. It also contains a sus4 chord. Try to create similar riffs with the voicings.

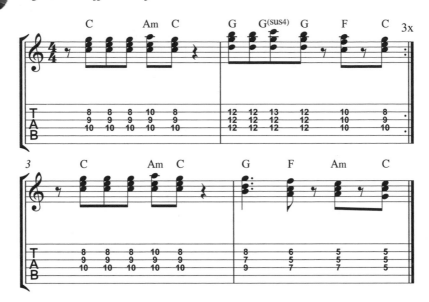

[Figure 135: Riff in C major]

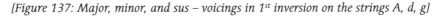

I will now show you the sus-voicings for strings A, d, and g. The voicings for strings E, A, and d are the same, but one string lower, respectively.

[Figure 136: Major, minor, and sus – voicings in root position on the strings A, d, g]

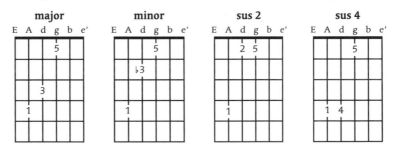

[Figure 137: Major, minor, and sus – voicings in 1st inversion on the strings A, d, g]

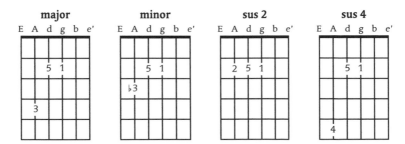

[Figure 138: Major, minor, and sus – voicings in 2nd inversion on the strings A, d, g]

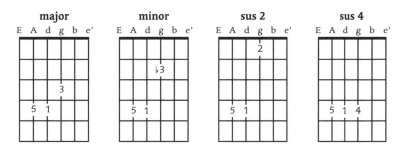

Not every chord in C which additionally contains a d is automatically a Csus2: if the voicing also contains the third, e, it is not replaced, but supplemented by the second. Such a chord is called a Cadd9 chord ('add' is short for 'additional'). A good example of such chords is the song Every Breath You Take' by the band The Police.

[Figure 139: The Police: Every Breath You Take]

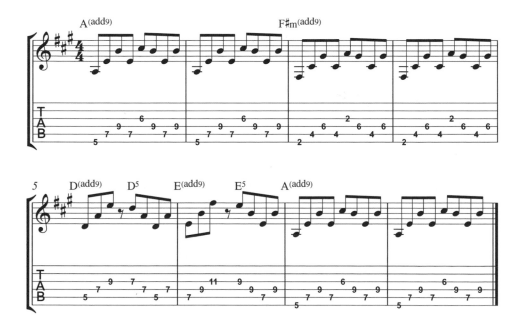

CHAPTER 7

Harmonization with Triads

In this chapter, I would like to demonstrate how easy melodies can be harmonized using the triads. Let's take a part of the well-known children's song Old MacDonald as an example.

In figure 140, you will see the melody in C major. For practicing, we will play the melody exclusively on the e-string. The chords C, F, and G are notated above the melody.

[Figure 140: Old MacDonald – Melody in C major]

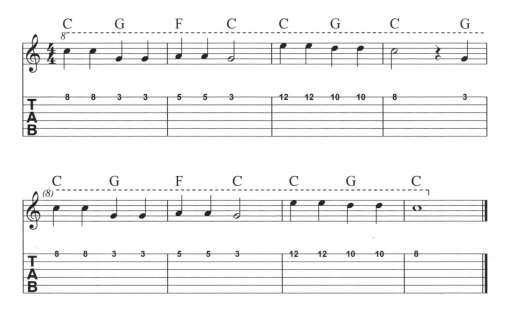

Let's have a look at the relationship between the notes of the melody and the corresponding chords.

- The 1st bar starts with the root of C major. Therefore, the corresponding C major chord has to carry the c in its melody part. We apply C major in its 1st inversion.

- On beat 3, the melody changes to g, which is the root of the corresponding G major chord. Therefore, we apply its 1st inversion.

- Measure 2 starts with an a. When we play F major in its 2nd inversion, we automatically get a as the top note.

- Now, the melody changes back to a g. C major is the matching chord. As the note g is the fifth in C major, we play it in its root position.

- In the 3rd measure, e is the top note. We harmonize it with the 2nd inversion of C major in order to keep the third in the melody part.

- Now the melody leads downwards to a d. We play a G major chord in its root position. This way, the fifth, d, is the top note.

- By playing the 1st inversion of C major, we get the root c at the beginning of bar 4 again. On beat 4, we have the note g, which we harmonize with the 1st inversion of G major, as before.

- Measures 5 to 8 are a repetition of the measures 1 to 4.

[Figure 141: Old MacDonald – harmonized in C major]

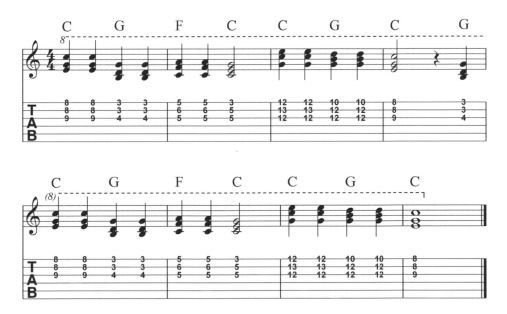

I have noted down the song in G major, too. Here, we play the melody on the b-string. The functions of the notes stay the same, only the fingerings change.

[Figure 142: Old MacDonald – Melody in G major]

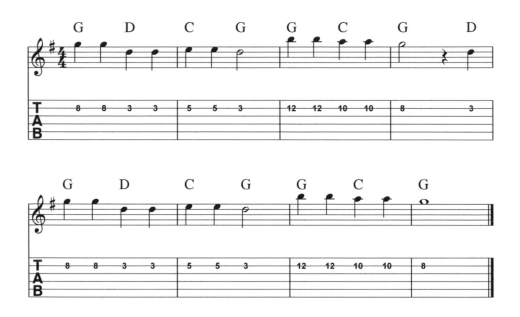

[Figure 143: Old MacDonald – harmonized in G major]

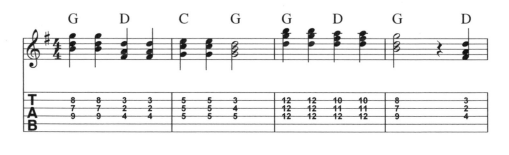

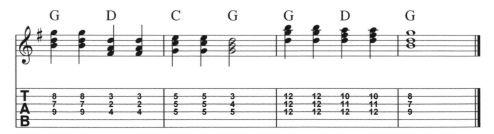

Try out this technique with songs of your choice. Make sure to choose easy songs at first. As an additional example, here is an arrangement of the song The Sound of Silence by Paul Simon.

[Figure 144: Paul Simon The Sound of Silence (Melody)]

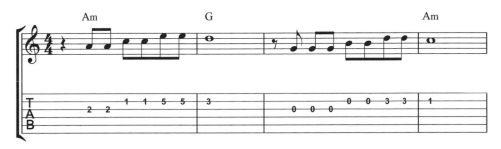

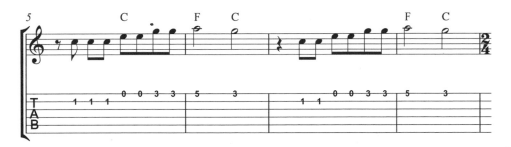

Here you see the song as a chord–melody arrangement.

[Figure 145: Paul Simon The Sound of Silence (chord–melody)]

As the song is written in C major (or A minor, respectively), we get the option of #11 for the subdominant F in measures 10 and 11. You will learn more about this in chapter 11. The following chapter provides more information on sixths in general and on the C6 chord in measure 12.

As you can see, triads are not only useful for rhythmical patterns and improvisation, but also for harmonization. Take the plunge and try out more difficult tonal material. Of course, you do not have to harmonize every note of the melody in three parts. It's enough to harmonize the chord changes and the stressed beats.

CHAPTER 8 I'm a Soulman: The Sixths

This chapter concentrates on one of the most interesting intervals, the so-called sixth, because the interval is the sixth note from the root. The song Soulman from the 1960's features some of these intervals in its introduction, which is absolutely fantastic. The sixth exists both as a minor (♭6, ♭13) and as a major interval (6, 13). Depending on the structure of the chord, the abbreviation '6' or '13' is used. The 13 designates the sixth shifted by an octave.

The sixth can sound like Hawaii, Christmas, rock, funk, blues or jazz, depending on its use. If we start with the root, c, the diatonic sixth is an a, which is a major sixth consisting of nine semitone steps. The minor sixth therefore is the note a♭ with eight semitone steps. Figure 146 shows the position of the major sixth in relation to the root, c, on the fretboard.

[Figure 146: Position of the major sixth in relation to the root c on the fretboard]

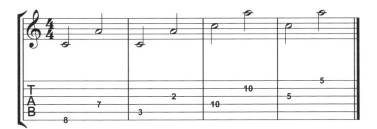

■ **Note:** If the root lies on the E– or on the A–string, the major sixth lies one fret lower and two strings higher (x–1). If the root lies on the d– or on the g–string, the major sixth lies two strings higher on the same fret, (x=x).

[Figure 147: Position of the major sixths (6) on the fretboard]

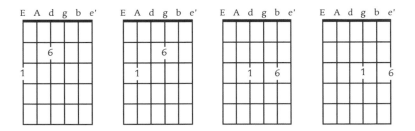

Of course, you can also find the major sixth two frets over the fifth on the next string, which would make four frets from the root, or five frets, if the root lies on the g–string.

When building sixths on all degrees of the major scale, you get major sixths on the degrees I, II, IV, and V. The remaining degrees, III, VI, and VII, form minor sixths. On the guitar, these are located on the next string (figure 148) or two strings higher (figure 149). Again, the root is c, its minor sixth being a♭.

[Figure 148: Position of the minor sixth a♭ in relation to the root c on the next string]

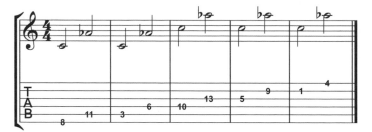

[Figure 149: Position of the minor sixth a♭ in relation to the root c two strings higher]

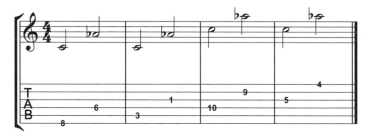

■ **Note:** If the root lies on the E– or on the A–string, the minor sixth lies two frets lower and two strings higher (x–2).

If the root lies on the d– or on the g–string, the minor sixth lies one fret lower and two strings higher (x–1).

If the root lies on the E–, A–, d–, or b– string, the minor sixth lies three frets higher on the next string (x+3).

If the root lies on the g–string, the minor sixth lies four frets higher on the b–string (x+4).

[Figure 150: Position of the minor sixths (♭6) on the fretboard]

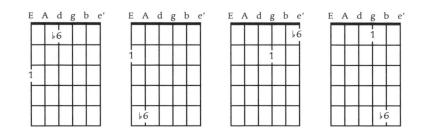

Figure 151 shows the diatonic sixths in G major. We start on the 5th fret of the d–string. When you want to play a sixth from the d– or the g–string, play the root with the middle finger and the minor sixth with the index finger. In order to get the major sixth, just play it with the ring finger on the same fret, placing it below the middle finger. If your root lies on the E– or on the A–string, play it with the middle finger again, and use your index finger for the sixths. For a minor sixth, you will have to stretch your index finger.

> **Tip:** Try hybrid picking: pluck the low string with the pick and the high string with the middle finger. This might take some time getting used to, but once you master this technique, you will love it!

[Figure 151: Diatonic sixths in G major]

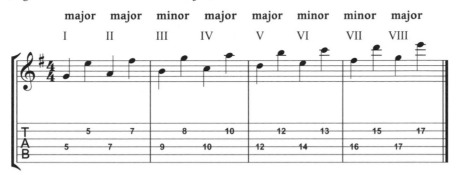

Figure 152 shows a line with diatonic sixths in 8th note triplets.

[Figure 152: Diatonic sixths in G major]

[Figure 153: Diatonic line of sixths in G major in 2–against–3 patterns]

Exercises on sixths

Play the diatonic sixths in the following keys and starting points horizontally on the fretboard (see figure 151). Play the exercise downwards, too!

C major (A–string 3rd fret / g-string 5th fret)
G major (E–string 3rd fret / open g-string)
D major (A–string 5th fret / open d-string, g-string 7th fret)
A major (E–string 5th fret / g–string 2nd fret)
E major (d–string 2nd fret)
B major (A–string 2nd fret / g–string 4th fret)
F major (E–string 1st fret / d–string 3rd fret)

Figure 154 shows how you can implement the sixth into a funk rock song, exercise is based around the style of Nuno Bettencourt. The guitarist from the band Extreme is one of funk rock's pioneers and an absolutely ingenious guitarist. The band's sound shaped the music of the late 80s.

[Figure 154: Funk rock riff with sixths]

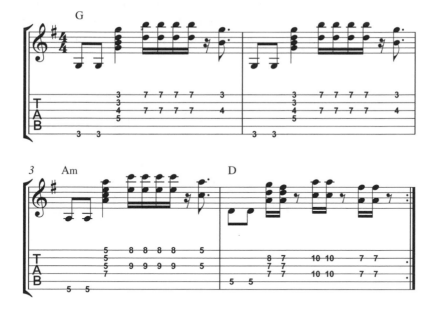

We use a G major chord played as a barre chord in the 1st two measures. On beat 3, play the major sixth, d''–b''; on beat 4a, play the minor sixth b'–g''. In the 3th measure (Am), we have a minor sixth first (beat 3, e''–c''), then a major one (beat 4a, c''–a'').

Another nice example is the song Belief by the singer and guitarist John Mayer. He has composed a great theme based on sixths.

[Figure 155: John Mayer: Belief]

Let's look at the sixth chords. The scheme of chord labeling is quite transparent: if a sixth or a minor sixth chord is indicated, you will have to play the conventional triad of the corresponding major or minor chord while adding a major sixth. Here I've given you just three or four fingerings for each type. This should be enough to cover the fretboard.

[Figure 156: 6th chords]

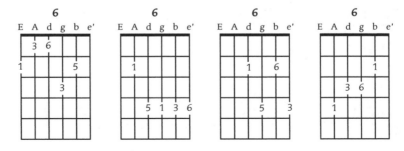

[Figure 157: m6 chords]

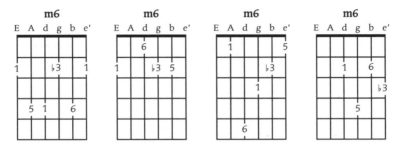

CHAPTER 9   Sevenths and Seventh Chords (Arpeggios)

In this chapter, we incorporate the sevenths into our repertoire. A seventh is the seventh note from the root. Just as for seconds, thirds, and sixths, there are major and minor versions of the seventh. The minor one carries the label '7', the major one maj7 (in chord symbols), or j7 (in interval and chord diagrams). The interval of the minor seventh comprises ten semitone steps, or 11 semitone steps for the major seventh. So, if the root is c, the major seventh is b.

In the historical development of harmony, the notes of a scale were numbered consecutively. Originally, the major seventh was labeled 7 and the minor seventh ♭7, just like the seconds, thirds, and sixths. But by and by, the labels changed to 7 for the minor seventh and maj7 for the major one.

[Figure 158: Position of the major seventh b in relation to the root c]

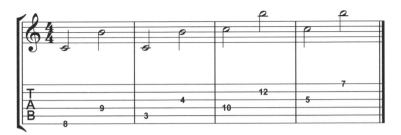

■ **Note:** If the root lies on the E– or on the A–string, you can find the major seventh one fret and two strings higher (x+1). If the root lies on the d– or on the g-string, the major seven is two frets and two strings higher (x+2).

Let's move on to the minor sevenths. The next figure shows the position of the minor seventh, b♭, in relation to the root, c.

[Figure 159: Position of the minor seventh b♭ in relation to the root c]

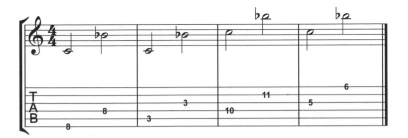

■ **Note:** If the root lies on the E– or on the A– string, you find the minor seventh two strings higher on the same fret (x=x). If the root lies on the d– or on the g– string, the minor sevenths lies one fret and two strings higher (x+1).

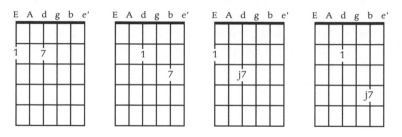

Below is a sample of a blues in A with the corresponding triads plus major sixths and minor sevenths.

[Figure 161: Blues line in A7]

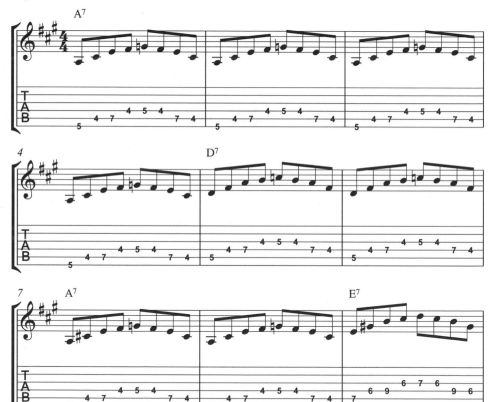

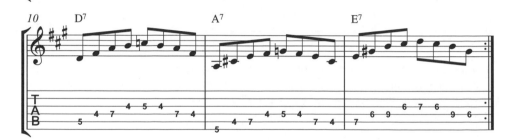

Figure 162 shows a typical riff which is often used in blues accompaniment (comping).

[Figure 162: Blues riff in A7]

The seventh sounds very bluesy when used in connection with the major triad and the sixth. In general, the interval of the seventh is tightly connected to blues and jazz. In each jazz standard, you will find mostly seventh chords.

If we extend a triad by another third, we get a seventh chord. This additional 4th note is the seventh of the root. Thus, a seventh chord consists of the following intervals: root–third–fifth–seventh. Within this chord, we have got many options to combine the major, minor, augmented and diminished intervals. However, we are going to limit the options to five types of seventh chords. First, we are going to have a look at their arpeggios.

9.1. The Major 7th chord (Arpeggios)

When we extend a major triad by a major third, we get a major 7th chord. The interval structure is as follows:

root	major third	fifth	major seventh	chord
c	e	g	b	Cmaj7

Major third + minor third + major third = major 7th chord (maj7)

In the major scale, you can find major 7th chords on degrees I and IV.

Let's have a look at the fretboard. You already know the positions of the triad arpeggios from chapter 4. The arpeggios end on the octave of the root. Here you can see the arpeggios distributed over three strings.

[Figure 163: major 7th arpeggios over 3 strings]

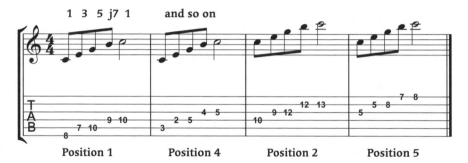

Position 1   Position 4   Position 2   Position 5

The next figure shows the major 7th arpeggios over 4 strings.

[Figure 164: major 7th arpeggios over 4 strings] [...and so on]

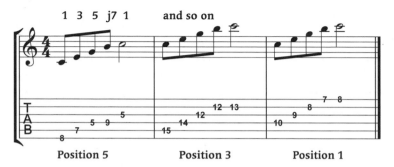

Position 5   Position 3   Position 1

You can, of course connect the arpeggios of figures 163 and 164 by taking the arpeggios of the same position. For example, you can combine measure 1 from figure 163 (position 1, three strings) with measure 3 from figure 164 (position 1, four strings). You can do the same with measure 1 from figure 164 (position 5, four strings) and measure 4 from figure 163 (position 5, three strings).

The following exercise demonstrates the combination of measure 1 (figure 163) and measure 3 (figure 164). It is notated down in sequences of three. Using such combinations, you prepare sequences like this more effectively than by just playing them upwards and downwards. In bars 3 and 4, you should play the sequence downwards, too.

Similarly, study the arpeggios of position 5.

[Figure 165: Exercise on Arpeggios: Cmaj7]

For fast patterns with movements through various octaves, symmetrical fingerings are best. The following arpeggios extend over two strings for each measure (figures 166–169).

When a chord contains four notes, there is of course one further inversion, making the seventh the lowest note (see figure 169).

[Figure 166: Cmaj7, root position]

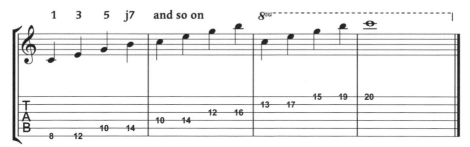

[Figure 167: Cmaj7, 1st inversion]

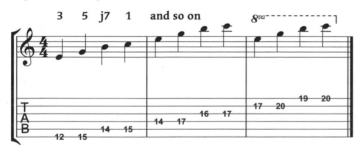

[Figure 168: Cmaj7, 2nd inversion]

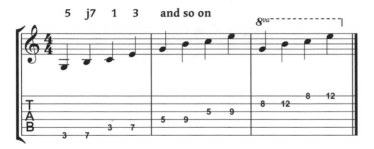

[Figure 169: Cmaj7, 3rd inversion]

Memorize the functions of the notes. This makes it easier to derive the arpeggios from this chapter.

Create your own exercises with arpeggios over two strings. You can take the exercise of figure 165 as an example. Practice it in 16th notes, too.

9.2. The Dominant 7th Chord (Arpeggios)

We obtain the dominant 7th chord by extending a major triad by a minor third. Thus, we have a major chord with an additional minor third.

The interval formula for a dominant 7th chord is:

root	major third	fifth	minor seventh	chord
c	e	g	b$\flat$	C7

Major third + minor third + minor third = dominant 7th chord

The dominant 7th chord is built on degree V of the major scale. In harmonic theory, it is one of the most important tools. Let's have a look at the G7 chord. The third b and the seventh f together form the interval of a diminished fifth. As you already know, this interval is full of tension and strives for resolution into the first degree of the scale, in this case, C major.

The third of the G7 chord, b, which is also called the guide note, moves a semitone upwards to c, the root of the tonic. The seventh of the G7, f, resolves into e, moving down a semitone to the third of the tonic. This is called a V–I progression.

[Figure 170: V–I progression G7 (third/seventh) to C (root/third)]

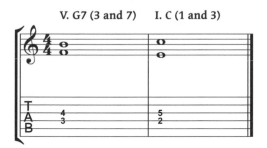

Now let's move on to the arpeggios. The seventh of the major 7th arpeggio from the preceding chapter gets flattened by a semitone. Try to keep this in mind while practicing.

[Figure 171: C dominant 7th arpeggio over 3 strings]

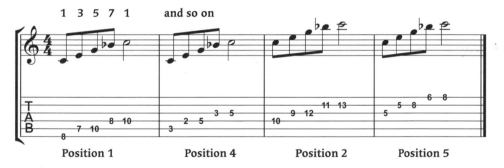

[Figure 172: C dominant 7th arpeggio over 4 strings]

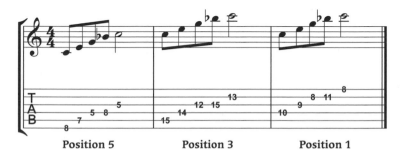

Try to combine the individual options. For example, you can combine measure 1 from figure 171 with measure 3 from figure 172, or measure 1 from figure 172 with measure 4 of figure 171. The individual indications for the positions on your fretboard might help you, as identical positions are easy to connect.

■ **Note:** In positions with two octaves, you can play two arpeggios or scales.
In position 1, play the fingering over three strings first, and from the octave on, change to the fingering over four strings.
In position 5, play the fingering over four strings first, and from the octave on, change to the fingering over three strings.
Of course, you can also do the same in the remaining three positions. However, here, the fingering does not expand over the complete octave.

Again, we have the arpeggios over two strings and in four variants, namely root position, 1st, 2nd, and 3rd inversions (see figures 173 – 176).

[Figure 173: C dominant 7th root position]

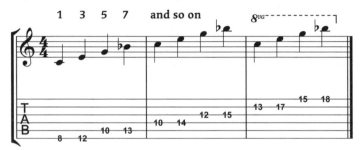

[Figure 174: C dominant 7th 1st inversion]

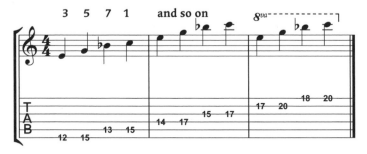

[Figure 175: C dominant 7th 2nd inversion]

[Figure 176: C dominant 7th 3rd inversion]

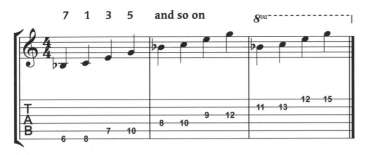

9.3. The Minor 7th Chord (Arpeggios)

We get a minor 7th chord, (m7 or –7), by expanding a minor triad by a minor third. These minor 7th chords can be built on the degrees II, III and VI of the major scale. The interval formula for minor 7th chords is:

root	minor third	fifth	minor seventh	chord
c	e♭	g	b♭	Cm7

minor third + major third + minor third = minor 7th chord

Compared with the dominant 7th chords, you now have to flatten the third by a semitone.

[Figure 177: Cm7 arpeggios over 3 strings]

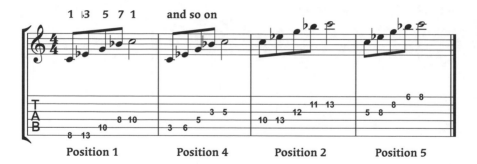

Position 1   Position 4   Position 2   Position 5

[Figure 178: Cm7 arpeggios over 4 strings]

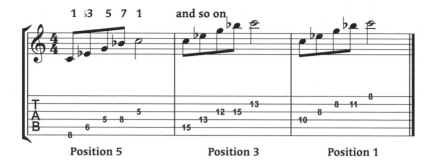

Position 5   Position 3   Position 1

You can easily connect Arpeggios of the same positions. Figures 179–182 give you four examples for minor 7th arpeggios over two strings. You can use them for quick lines.

[Figure 179: Cm7 root position]

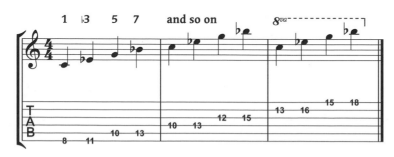

[Figure 180: Cm7 1st inversion]

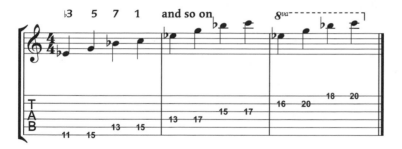

[Figure 181: Cm7 2nd inversion]

[Figure 182: Cm7 3rd inversion]

9.4. The m7♭5 (half diminished) Chord (Arpeggios)

You get the m7♭5 chord, or half diminished chord, by expanding a diminished triad by a major third. The m7♭5 chord is built on the degree VII of the major scale. The '♭5' in the label of the chord refers to the diminished fifth in the chord structure; thus, it is a minor 7th chord with a diminished fifth. Its interval structure is:

root	minor third	dim. fifth	minor seventh	chord
c	e♭	g♭	b♭	Cm7♭5

Minor third + minor third + major third = m7♭5 chord

In major chord progressions, the m7♭5 chord is quite rare. In contrast, it has an important role in minor progressions, but we will learn about this later.

[Figure 183: Cm7♭5 arpeggio over 3 strings]

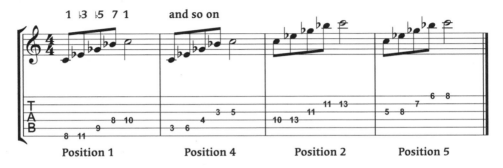

[Figure 184: Cm7♭5 arpeggio over 4 strings]

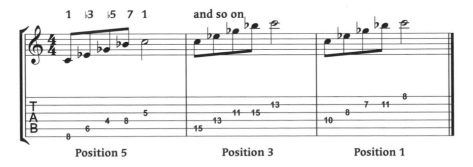

Figures 185 to 188 show arpeggios over two strings in root position and all inversions. They come in handy if you want to play across several octaves quickly.

[Figure 185: Cm7♭5 root position]

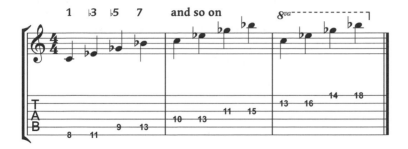

[Figure 186: Cm7♭5 1st inversion]

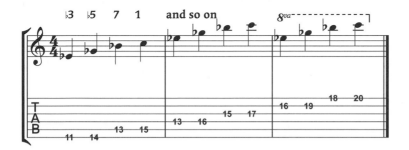

[Figure 187: Cm7♭5 2nd inversion]

[Figure 188: Cm7♭5 3rd inversion]

9.5. The Diminished 7th chord (Arpeggios)

The diminished 7th, (dim7, °7), or fully diminished chord, holds a special position as it consists of three minor thirds. This means that a diminished triad is expanded by a minor third. As the resulting seventh lies one semitone below the minor seventh, we also speak of a diminished seventh. In our example with the root, c, the seventh b♭ is flattened to b♭♭.

The interval structure for this diminished 7th chord is:

root	minor third	dim. fifth	dim. seventh	chord
c	e♭	g♭	b♭♭	C°7

Minor third + minor third + minor third = °7 chord (diminished 7th)

Also the distance between the diminished 7th and the octave of the root is a minor third. This is the reason why the arpeggio is symmetrical: It consists of a sequence of minor thirds and repeats itself every three frets. In this diminished 7th chord, each note can take on every function, depending on the chosen root.

The chord is used on the degree VII of the harmonic minor scale. Neoclassical guitarists such as Yngwie Malmsteen use it frequently.

[Figure 189: Cdim7 arpeggio]

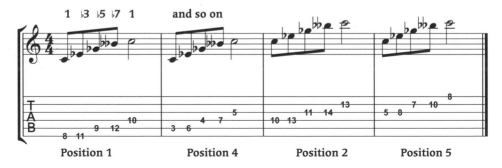

Figures 190–193 show the root position and inversions distributed on two strings.

[Figure 190: Cdim7 root position]

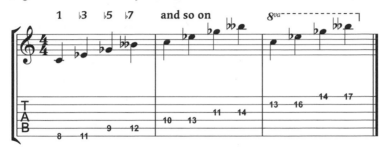

[Figure 191: Cdim7 1st inversion]

[Figure 192: Cdim7 2nd inversion]

[Figure 193: Cdim7 3rd inversion]

9.6. Exercises on 7th chords (Arpeggios)

Let's look at the concept which helps you put all this material to practical use. For this, we will take a part of a slightly modified jazz standard called Autumn Leaves. The chord progression is:

Chord	Am7	D7	Gmaj7	Cmaj7	F#m7♭5	B7	Em7	E7
Degree	II	V	I	IV	II	V	I	SD
Key	G major				E minor			

In the first four measures of each exercise, you will find a major II–V–I–IV progression. In measure 5–7, the II–V–I progression is minor. The E7 in the last measure is a secondary dominant and leads back to Am7 in the first measure. Degree V of the minor cadence gets the additional ♭9 most times. You will learn more about this in chapter 12.

34-35

Exercise 1
On the CD, you will find the playbacks on tracks 34 (116 bpm) and 35 (154 bpm). First, find roots on the fretboard that interlock logically, that is those positioned on neighboring strings. We start with Am7 on the E-string on the 5th fret. Figure 194 indicates the roots for exercise 1.

[Figure 194: Exercise 1 – roots of the arpeggios]

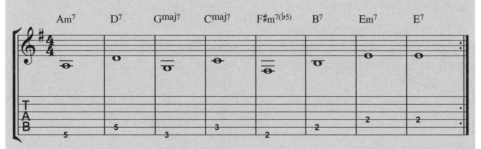

Now, play the arpeggios and stop at the octave of the root.

[Figure 195: Exercise 1 – ascending arpeggios]

Next, play the arpeggios ascending and descending.

[Figure 196: Exercise 1 – arpeggios in straight 8th notes]

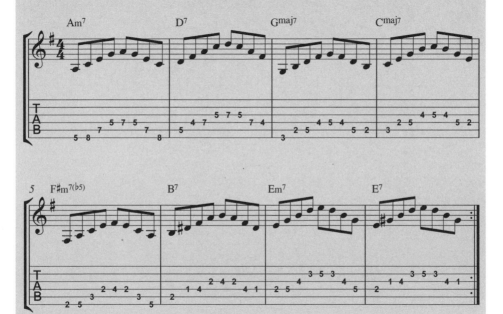

Now try to take the shortest route between the notes of the chords when changing. Thus, measures 3 and 4 change. Play the Cmaj7 downwards and beyond the octave area. The note a on beat 4 has been inserted for a smoother melody line, and it is not part of Cmaj7.

[Figure 197: Exercise 1 – arpeggios with enhanced melody line]

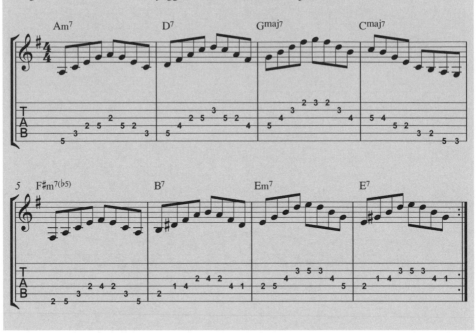

Exercise 2

The following exercise starts at the next position of the note, a, which is position 2 (d–string, 7th fret). First, the roots:

[Figure 198: Exercise 2 – roots of the arpeggios]

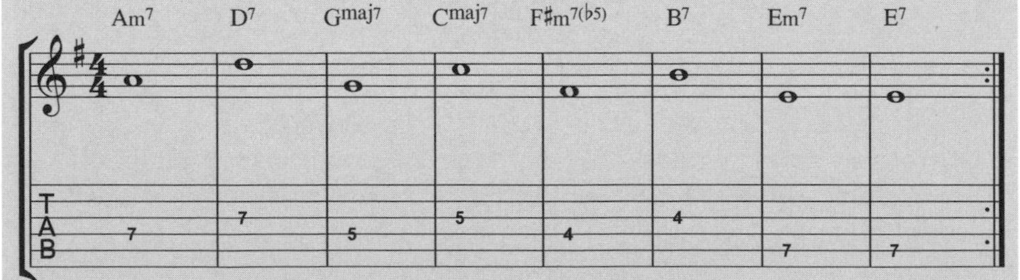

Now play the arpeggios upwards until you reach the root again (transposed by an octave).

[Figure 199: Exercise 2 – ascending arpeggios]

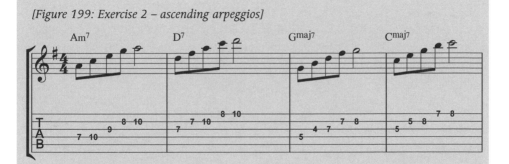

We have straight 8th notes again.

[Figure 200: Exercise 2 – arpeggios in straight 8th notes]

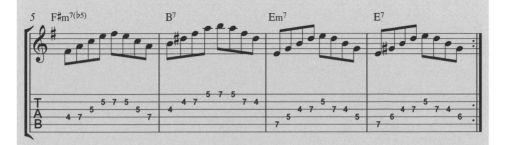

Try to find logical connections by using different fingerings.

Exercise 3

The next exercise starts on position 3 of the note, a, on the 12th fret of the A–string. Now, we use 8th notes straight from the beginning:

[Figure 201: Exercise 3 – Arpeggios in straight 8th notes]

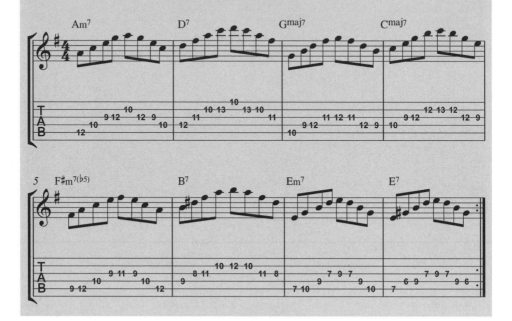

Exercise 4

In figure 202, we start at position 4 of Am7.

[Figure 202: Exercise 4 – Arpeggios in straight 8ᵗʰ notes]

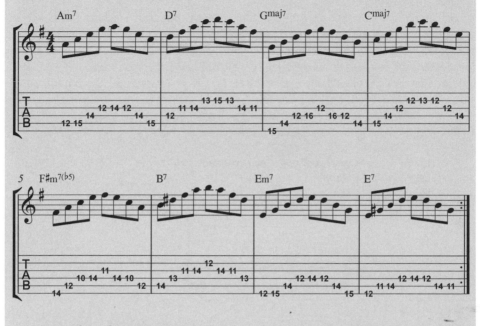

Transpose these four excercises to the keys heard on the CD (tracks 36–41). The corresponding chord progressions can be found in the appendix.

36-41

I recommend acquiring a Real Book. With this 'jazz musician's bible' and the system you have just learned, you will accomplish fluent playing without having to think and search too much. There is no other type of music collection offering so many songs with seventh chords. If you practice the songs as recommended in the last few steps, your overview of the fretboard and your arpeggio playing are going to improve quickly. Always look for the ideal fingering of the arpeggios without switching positions too much.

CHAPTER 10

Seventh Chord Voicings

10.1 Drop3 Voicings

Drop3 – Root Position

Now that you are able to construct different seventh chords by stacking thirds, we are going to have a look at the resulting fingerings. Due to the tuning of the guitar, the system of root position chords and inversions only works in part. For guitarists, a different scheme for creating the voicings is more suitable, which is called 'Drop3'. Here, the 3rd highest note of the voicing is played one octave lower. Let's have a look at this system in root position. This voicing would still be playable.

[Figure 203: Drop3 voicing in root position (rp)]

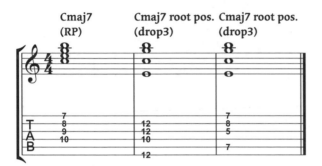

As you can see in the notes, the third e is set one octave lower in the 2nd and 3rd measure. In order to be able to play the voicings, the notes are set on a different fretboard area. In drop3 voicings, one string is skipped between the bass note and the remaining notes. This way, we get the root position of the drop3 voicing. This means that the seventh of the chord is in the melody part. The third of the chord lies in the bass.

In the following two figures, you can see the chords notated in chord diagrams. By modifying the thirds, fifths, and sevenths, you will get the desired chord type (maj7, 7, m7, m7♭5). The dim7 chords will be treated separately in chapter 10.3.

[Figure 204: Drop3 chords in root position on the strings E–d–g–b]

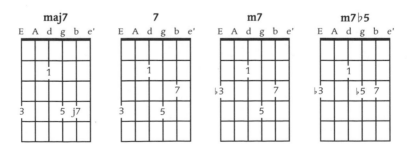

[Figure 205: Drop3 chords in root position on the strings A–g–b–e']

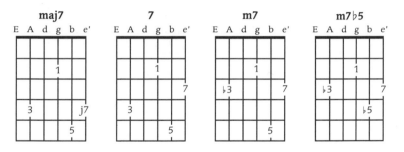

■ **Note:** In drop3 voicings in root position, the seventh lies in the melody part and the third lies in the bass. The root and fifth build the middle parts. For the following exercises, it is important to memorize which note of the chord builds the bass part.

As you can see, the chord diagrams for the strings E–A–d–g and A–g–b–e' are the same. In order to play the voicings on the strings A–g–b–e', you only have to play the note on the b–string one fret higher.

Drop3 – 2nd inversion

In the 2nd inversion of the chord, the third is the top part. The seventh (second lowest note of the voicing) is shifted one octave lower and takes over the bass part.

[Figure 206: Drop3 voicings in the 2nd inversion]

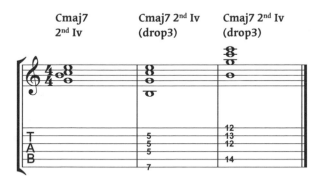

[Figure 207: Drop3 voicings in 2nd inversion on the strings E–d–g–b]

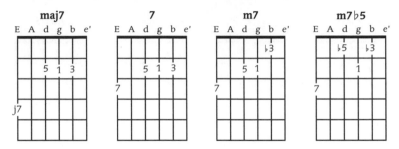

[Figure 208: Drop3 voicings in 2nd inversion on the strings A–g–b–e']

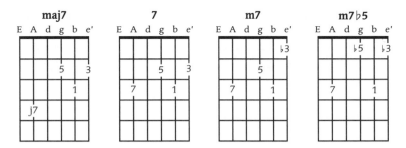

■ **Note:** In drop3 voicings in 2nd inversion, the third is in the melody, whereas the seventh takes the bass part. The root and fifth are in the middle.

In a close voicing, the chords of a cadence alternate between the root position and the 2nd inversion. Therefore, when you start the cadence with a voicing in root position, you need the 2nd inversion for the following chord, and vice versa.

Exercises on drop3 voicings (root position and 2nd inversion)

Exercise 1

Here are some exercises which will help you to implement these voicings. The exercises consist of II–V–I progressions in major and minor. First is the chord progression with alternating root position and 2nd inversion in major.

[Figure 209: IIm7 – V7 – Imaj7 drop3 voicings on the strings E–d–g–b]

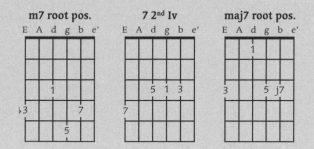

[Figure 210: IIm7 – V7 – Imaj7 drop3 voicings on the strings A–g–b–e']

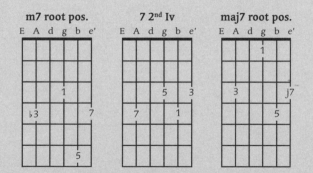

Sample chord progression: Dm7 – G7 – Cmaj7

▷ Determine the root position of Dm7 (the third is in the bass!). You have to play the third, f, on the 13th fret, in accordance to figure 209. In figure 210, you will find the third, f, on the 8th fret.

▷ Play the chord.

▷ Determine the 2nd inversion of G7. In 2nd inversion, the seventh lies in the bass. For G7, this would be the note f, which can keep its position.

▷ Play the chord.

▷ Determine the root position of Cmaj7. The bass note is now the third, e, on the 12th fret (figure 209) or on the 7th fret (figure 210).

⇨ Play the chord.

⇨ Practice the chord progression for the strings E–d–g–b.

⇨ Practice the chord progression for the strings A–g–b–e'.

⇨ Transfer the fingering change into the following II–V–I progressions:
Am7 – D7 – Gmaj7
Cm7 – F7 – B♭maj7
Gm7 – C7 – Fmaj7

⇨ Practice the fingering changes with the bass notes on the E– and on the A– string, respectively.

Exercise 2
In the next exercise we will practice the voicings starting in the 2nd inversion.

[Figure 211: IIm7 – V7 – Imaj7 Drop3 voicings on the strings E-d-g-b]

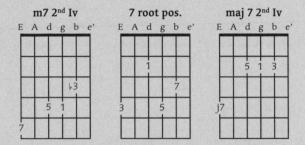

[Figure 212: IIm7 – V7 – Imaj7 Drop3 voicings on the strings A-g-b-e']

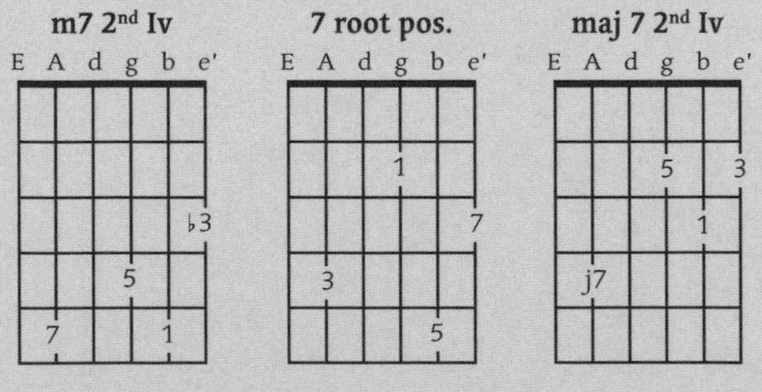

126

Sample chord progression: Dm7 – G7 – Cmaj7

↪ Determine the 2nd inversion of Dm7: the seventh is in the bass. Therefore, you have to play the seventh, c, on the 8th fret, as shown in figure 211. In figure 212 you will find the seventh, c, on the 3rd or on the 15th fret, respectively.

↪ Play the chord.

↪ Determine the root position of G7. The third is in the bass (see figure 211, 7th fret, figure 212, 2nd or 14th fret).

↪ Play the chord.

↪ Determine the 2nd inversion of Cmaj7. The bass note, b, is already in the bass (figure 211, 7th fret, figure 212, 2nd or 14th fret, respectively)

↪ Play the chord.

↪ Practice the chord progression for the strings E–d–g–b.

↪ Practice the chord progression for the strings A–g–b–e'.

↪ Transfer the changes to the following II – V – I progressions:
Am7 – D7 – Gmaj7
Cm7 – F7 – B♭maj7
Gm7 – C7 – Fmaj7

↪ Practice the changes with the bass notes on the E- and A-strings.

Exercise 3
Let's look at the II – V – I progression in minor. For this chord progression, we start in root position again.

[Figure 213: IIm7♭5 – V7 – Im7 drop3 voicings on the strings E–d–g–b]

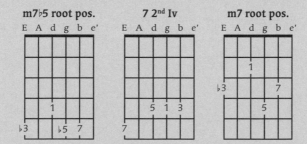

Now fill in the correct progression for the voicings for the strings A–g–b–e' in figure 214 on your own. You will find the solution in the appendix.

*[Figure 214: **Task 1:** IIm7♭5 – V7 – Im7 drop3 voicings on the strings A–G–b–e']*

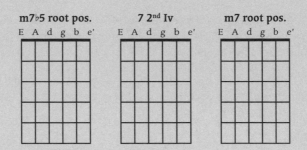

m7♭5 root pos.	**7 2ⁿᵈ Iv**	**m7 root pos.**
E A d g b e'	E A d g b e'	E A d g b e'

Sample chord progression: Em7♭5 – A7 – Dm7

↪ Determine the root position of Em7♭5. The third, g, is the bass note (see figure 213: 3ʳᵈ or 15ᵗʰ fret; figure 214: 10ᵗʰ fret)

↪ Play the chord

↪ Determine the 2ⁿᵈ inversion of A7. The seventh, g, is the bass note and can remain the same.

↪ Play the chord.

↪ Determine the root position of Dm7. The third, f, is the bass note (see figure 213: 1ˢᵗ or 13ᵗʰ fret; figure 214, 8ᵗʰ fret).

↪ Play the chord.

↪ Practice the chord progression for the strings E, d, g, b.

↪ Practice the chord progression for the strings A, g, b, e'.

↪ Now, transfer the fingering changes to the following IIm7♭5 – V7 – Im7 progressions:
F#m7♭5 – B7 – Em7
Bm7♭5 – E7 – Am7
Am7♭5 – D7 – Gm7

↪ Also practice the fingering changes with the bass notes on the E– as well as on the A– string.

Exercise 4

In exercise 4, we start the chord progression with the voicing in 2nd inversion.

[Figure 215: IIm7b5 – V7 – Im7 drop3 voicings on the strings E–d–g–b]

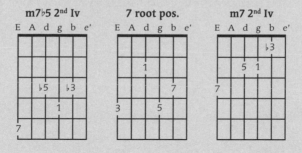

Task 2: Fill in the voicings for the strings A–g–b–e' in figure 216, yourself.

[Figure 216: Task 2: IIm7b5 – V7 – Im7 drop3 voicings on the strings A–g–b–e']

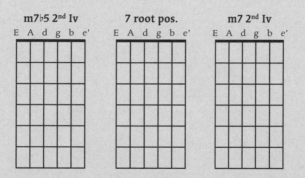

Sample chord progression: Em7b5 – A7 – Dm7

⇨ Determine the 2nd inversion of Em7b5. The seventh, d, is the bass note
  (see figure 215, 10th fret, figure 216, 5th fret)

⇨ Play the chord.

⇨ Determine the root position of A7. The third, c#, is the bass note
  (Figure 215, 9th fret, figure 216, 4th fret).

⇨ Play the chord.

⇨ Determine the 2nd inversion of Dm7. The seventh, c, is the bass note
  (see figure 215, 8th fret, figure 216, 3rd fret)

⇨ Play the chord.

⇨ Practice the chord progression for the strings E, d, g, b.

⇨ Practice the chord progression for the strings A, g, b, e'.

⇨ Now, transfer the fingering changes to the following IIm7♭5 – V7 – Im7 progressions:
F#m7♭5 – B7 – Em7
Bm7♭5 – E7 – Am7
Am7♭5 – D7 – Gm7

⇨ Also practice the chord changes with the bass notes on the E– as well as on the A–string.

34-35

Exercise 5
Sample chord progression: Am7 – D7 – Gmaj7 – Cmaj7 – F#m7♭5 – B7 – Em7 – E7

⇨ Start with the first chord in its 2nd inversion. The 2nd chord takes on the root position, and so on.

⇨ Now, determine the bass notes. Remember: In 2nd inversion, the seventh is in the bass, and in the root position, the third is in the bass.

[Figure 217: Exercise 5: bass line]

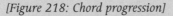

Play the chord progression with the complete voicings along with the playback (track 34: slow; track 35: medium).

[Figure 218: Chord progression]

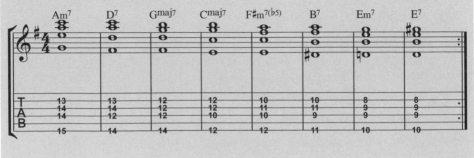

Repeat the exercise with the following chord progressions:
Dm7 – G7 – Cmaj7 – Fmaj7 – Bm7♭5 – E7 – Am7 – A7 [CD track 36/37]
Gm7 – C7 – Fmaj7 – B♭maj7 – Em7♭5 – A7 – Dm7 – D7 [CD track 38/39]
Cm7 – F7 – B♭maj7 – E♭maj7 – Am7♭5 – D7 – Gm7 – G7 [CD track 40/41]

36/37
38/39
40/41

Exercise 6

36/37

Sample chord progression: Dm7 – G7 – Cmaj7 – Fmaj7 – Bm7♭5 – E7 – Am7 – A7

⇨ Start with the first chord in its root position.

⇨ Now, determine the bass line for the whole progression. Remember: In root position, the third is in the bass and in the 2nd inversion, the seventh is in the bass!

[Figure 219: Exercise 6: bass line]

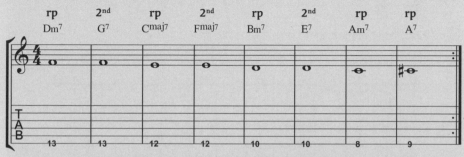

⇨ Play the chord progression along with the playback (CD tracks 36/37).

[Figure 220: Chord progression]

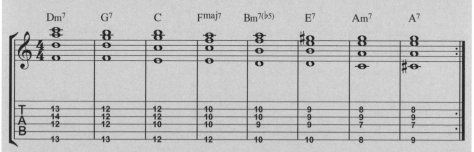

Repeat this exercise with the following chord progressions:
Am7 – D7 – Gmaj7 – Cmaj7 – F#m7♭5 – B7 – Em7 – E7 [CD tracks 34/35]
Gm7 – C7 – Fmaj7 – B♭maj7 – Em7♭5 – A7 – Dm7 – D7 [CD tracks 38/39]
Cm7 – F7 – B♭maj7 – E♭maj7 – Am7♭5 – D7 – Gm7 – G7 [CD tracks 40/41]

34/35
38/39
40/41

Drop3 – 1st inversion

Now, let's have a look at this system using the 1st inversion of the Cmaj7 chord. This voicing cannot be played with the guitar's regular tuning, which is why we have to switch to drop3 voicings. Here, the root (or octave) lies in the melody part and the fifth in the bass part (1st inversion).

[Figure 221: Drop3 voicing in 1st inversion]

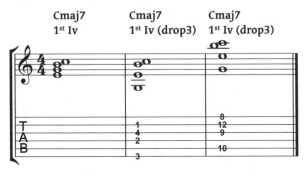

[Figure 222: Drop3 voicings in 1st inversion on the strings E–d–g–b]

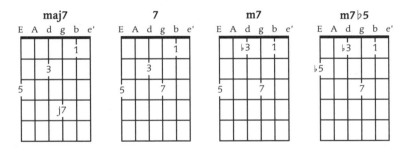

[Figure 223: Drop3 voicings in 1st inversion on the strings A–g–b–e']

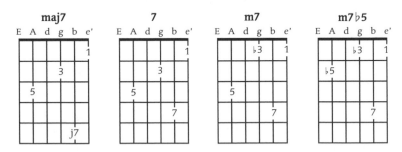

■ **Note:** In drop3 voicings in 1st inversion, the root always lies in the melody part and the fifth is the bass note. The third and the seventh form the middle parts.

Drop3 Voicing – 3rd Inversion

In the 3rd inversion of a seventh chord, the fifth lies in the melody part and the root forms the bass note.

[Figure 224: Drop3 voicing in 3rd inversion]

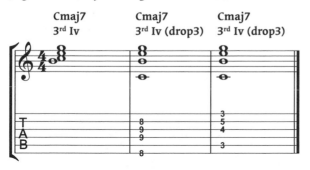

[Figure 225: Drop3 voicings in root position on the strings E–d–g–b]

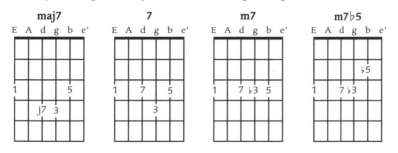

[Figure 226: Drop3 voicings in root position on the strings A–g–b–e']

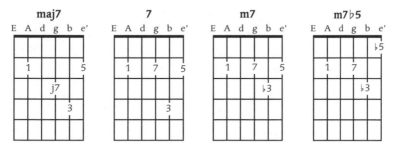

■ **Note:** In drop3 voicings in 3rd inversion, the fifth always lies in the melody part and the root is the bass note. The third and the seventh form the middle parts.

In a close voicing, the inverted chords of a cadence alternate. Thus, if you start a cadence with a voicing in 3rd inversion, you need the 1st inversion for the following chord and vice versa.

Exercises on 1st and 3rd inversion in drop3 voicings

Exercise 1

Here are six exercises on voicings in 3rd and 1st inversion. Again, it is all about II – V – I progressions. We start with the major progression, and the first chord is in its 3rd inversion.

[Figure 227: IIm7 – V7 – Imaj7 Drop3 voicings on the strings E–d–g–b]

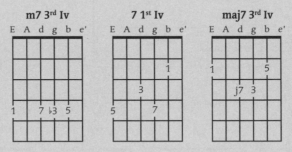

Try inserting the voicings for the strings A–g–b–e' on your own **(Task 3)**. You will find the solution in the appendix.

[Figure 228: Task 3: IIm7 – V7 – Imaj7 Drop3 voicings on the strings E–d–g–b]

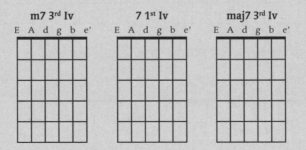

Sample chord progression: Dm7 – G7 – Cmaj7

↪ Determine the 3rd inversion of Dm7. The root is in the bass (figure 227, 10th fret, figure 228, 5th fret)

↪ Determine the 1st inversion of G7. The fifth forms the bass. Therefore, the bass of the preceding voicing can stay the same.

↪ Determine the 3rd inversion of Cmaj7. The root is in the bass (figure 227, 8th fret, figure 228, 3rd fret).

↪ Practice the chord progression on the strings E–d–g–b.

⇨ Practice the chord progression on the strings A–g–b–e'.

⇨ Transfer the fingerings into the following II – V – I progressions:
Am7 – D7 – Gmaj7
Cm7 – F7 – B♭maj7
Gm7 – C7 – Fmaj7

⇨ Practice the chord progressions with the bass note on the E– and on the A–string.

Exercise 2

In the next exercise we start with the first chord in its 1st inversion.

[Figure 229: IIm7 – V7 – Imaj7 Drop3 voicings on the strings E–d–g–b]

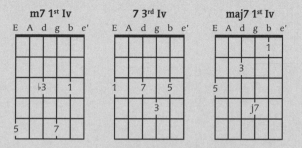

Task 4: Insert the voicings for the strings A–g–b–e' on your own.

[Figure 230: IIm7 – V7 – Imaj7 Drop3 voicings on the strings A–g–b–e']

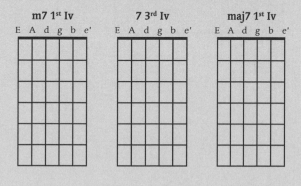

Sample chord progression: Dm7 – G7 – Cmaj7

⇨ Determine the 1st inversion of Dm7. The fifth, a is in the bass (figure 229, 5th fret, figure 230, 12th fret)

⇨ Determine the 3rd inversion of G7. The root forms the bass (figure 229, 3rd fret, figure 230, 10th fret).

⇨ Determine the 1st inversion of Cmaj7. The fifth, g is in the bass and can remain the same as in the preceding chord.

⇨ Practice the chord progression on the strings E–d–g–b.

⇨ Practice the chord progression on the strings A–g–b–e'.

⇨ Transfer the fingerings to the following II – V – I progressions:
Am7 – D7 – Gmaj7
Cm7 – F7 – B♭maj7
Gm7 – C7 – Fmaj7

⇨ Practice the chord progressions with the bass note on the E– and on the A–string.

Exercise 3
In exercise 3, I will show you the fingering changes within a minor II – V – I progression. We start with the first chord in its 3rd inversion.

[Figure 231: IIm7♭5 – V7 – Im7 Drop3 voicings on the strings E–d–g–b]

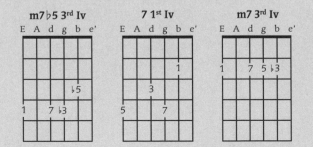

Task 5: Insert the chord diagrams for the strings A–g–b–e' yourself.

[Figure 232: Task 5: IIm7♭5 – V7 – Im7 Drop3 voicings on the strings A–g–b–e']

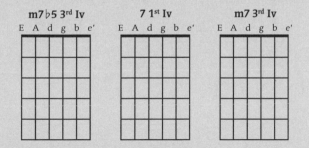

Sample chord progression: Em7♭5 – A7 – Dm7

↪ Determine the 3rd inversion of Em7♭5. The root is in the bass (figure 231, 12th fret, figure 232, 7th fret)

↪ Determine the 1st inversion of A7. The fifth, e, forms the bass and can remain the same as in the preceding voicing.

↪ Determine the 3rd inversion of Dm7. The root is in the bass (figure 231, 10th fret, figure 232, 5th fret)

↪ Practice the chord progression on the strings E–d–g–b.

↪ Practice the chord progression on the strings A–g–b–e'.

↪ Transfer the fingerings to the following IIm7♭5 – V7 – Im7 progressions:
F#m7♭5 – B7 – Em7
Bm7♭5 – E7 – Am7
Am7♭5 – D7 – Gmaj7

↪ Practice the chord progressions with the bass note on the E– and on the A–string.

Exercise 4

The following exercise starts with the first chord in its 1st inversion.

[Figure 233: IIm7♭5 – V7 – Im7 Drop3 voicings on the strings E–d–g–b]

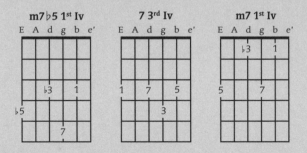

Task 6: Insert the chord diagrams for the strings A–g–b–e' yourself.

[Figure 234: IIm7♭5 – V7 – Im7 Drop3 voicings on the strings A–g–b–e']

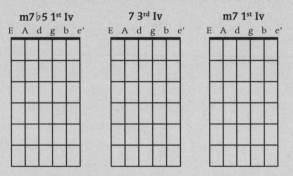

Sample chord progression: Em7♭5 – A7 – Dm7

➪ Determine the 1st inversion of Em7♭5. The fifth, b♭, is in the bass (figure 233: 6th fret; figure 234: 13th fret).

➪ Determine the 3rd inversion of A7. The root forms the bass (figure 233: 5th fret, figure 234, 12th fret).

➪ Determine the 1st inversion of Dm7. The fifth, a, is in the bass and can stay the same as in the preceding chord.

➪ Practice the chord progression on the strings E–d–g–b.

➪ Practice the chord progression on the strings A–g–b–e'.

➪ Transfer the fingerings into the following IIm7♭5 – V7 – Im7 progressions:
F#m7♭5 – B7 – Em7
Bm7♭5 – E7 – Am7
Am7♭5 – D7 – Gm7

➪ Practice the chord progresssions with the bass note on the E– and A–strings.

138

Exercise 5

Sample chord progression: Dm7 – G7 – Cmaj7 – Fmaj7 – Bm7♭5 – E7 – Am7 – A7

▷ Start with the first chord in its 3rd inversion. The second chord is built in 1st inversion, and so on.

▷ Now, determine the bass note: In 3rd inversion, the root is in the bass and in the 1st inversion the fifth is in the bass.

[Figure 235: Exercise 5 – bass part]

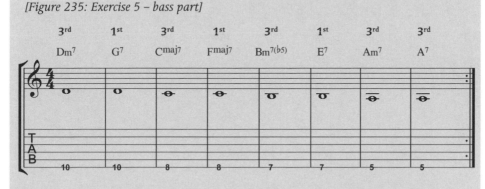

Play the chord progression along with the playback (track 36: slow; track 37: medium).

[Figure 236: Chord progression]

Repeat the exercise for the chord progression in the following keys:
Am7 – D7 – Gmaj7 – Cmaj7 – F#m7♭5 – B7 – Em7 – E7 [CD tracks 34/35]
Gm7 – C7 – Fmaj7 – B♭maj7 – Em7♭5 – A7 – Dm7 – D7 [CD tracks 38/39]
Cm7 – F7 – B♭maj7 – E♭maj7 – Am7♭5 – D7 – Gm7 – G7 [CD tracks 40/41]

34/35
38/39
40/41

Exercise 6

Sample chord progression: Am7 – D7 – Gmaj7 – Cmaj7 – F#m7♭5 – B7 – Em7 – E7

⇨ Start with the first chord in its 1st inversion. The second chord is built in its 3rd inversion, and so on.

⇨ Now, determine the bass notes. Remember: In the 1st inversion, the fifth is in the bass and in the 3rd inversion, the root is in the bass!

[Figure 237: Bass part]

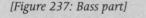

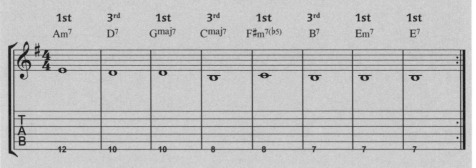

Play the chord progression along with the playback (track 34: slow; track 35: medium).

[Figure 238: Chord progression]

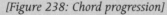

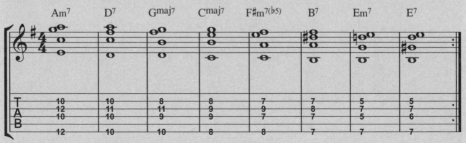

Repeat the exercise for the chord progression in the following keys:
Dm7 – G7 – Cmaj7 – Fmaj7 – Bm7♭5 – E7 – Am7 – A7 [CD tracks 36/37]
Gm7 – C7 – Fmaj7 – B♭maj7 – Em7♭5 – A7 – Dm7 – D7 [CD tracks 38/39]
Cm7 – F7 – B♭maj7 – E♭maj7 – Am7♭5 – D7 – Gm7 – G7 [CD tracks 40/41]

10.2. Drop2 Voicings

Drop2 – Root Position

The drop2 voicing system offers a further (and equally important) option in building seventh chords. Here, the 2nd highest note of the root position (or of the inversions) is set one octave lower. This way, the root position of the Cmaj7 chord (c–e–g–b) is modified to (G–c–e–b). In contrast to drop3 voicings, drop2 voicings are built on neighboring strings. In the root position of drop2 voicings, the fifth lies in the bass.

[Figure 239: Drop2 voicings in root position (fifth in the bass)]

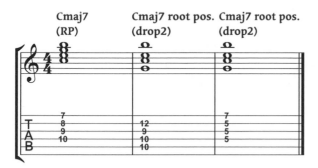

Drop2 voicings can be played in three variants:
on the strings A–d–g–b
on the strings d–g–b–e'
on the strings E–a–d–g

I've left out the option of playing it on the four lowest strings, as the resulting sound is quite muffled.

Here I show you the voicings on the strings A–d–g–b.

[Figure 240: Drop2 Voicings (root position) on the strings A–d–g–b]

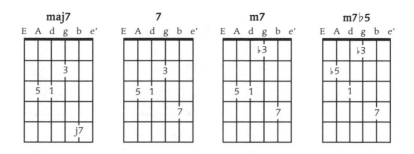

Here you can see the voicings of the root position on the strings d–g–b–e'.

[Figure 241: Drop2 Voicings (root position) on the strings d–g–b–e']

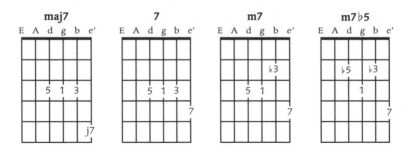

■ **Note:** In drop2 voicings in root position, the seventh lies in the melody part and the fifth is in the bass. The root and the third form the middle parts.

Drop2 – 2nd inversion

In the 2nd inversion of the drop2 voicing, the third of the chord is in the melody part. The root is set one octave lower and takes the bass part.

[Figure 242: Drop2 Voicings in 2nd inversion (root in the bass)]

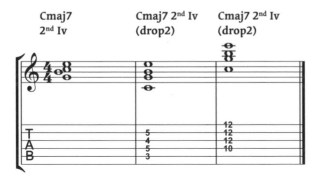

The following figures show the voicings on the strings A–d–g–b and d–g–b–e'.

[Figure 243: Drop2 Voicings in 2nd inversion on the strings A–d–g–b]

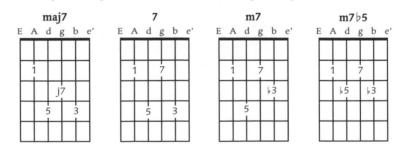

[Figure 244: Drop2 Voicings in 2nd inversion on the strings d–g–b–e']

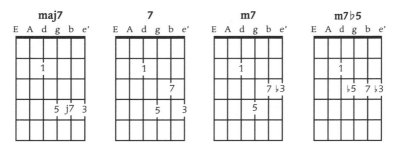

■ **Note:** In drop2 voicings in 2nd inversion, the third is in the melody part and the root forms the bass. The fifth and seventh take the middle parts.

In close voicings, the positions of the chords of a cadence alternate. If you start the cadence with a voicing in root position, the next chord is formed in 2nd inversion, and vice versa.

Exercises on the Drop2 voicings in root position and 2nd inversion

Exercise 1

Here are exercises implementing drop2 voicings in root position and 2nd inversion, below. The first exercises are based on major II – V – I progressions. We start with the first chord in its root position.

[Figure 245: IIm7 – V7 – Imaj7 Drop2 voicings on the strings A–d–g–b]

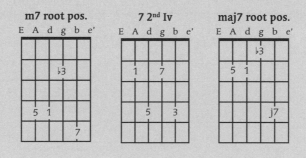

Task 7: Insert the voicings for the chord progression on the strings d–g–b–e' yourself. Start with the root position. You will find the solution in the appendix.

[Figure 246: Task 7: IIm7 – V7 – Imaj7 Drop2 voicings on the strings d–g–b–e']

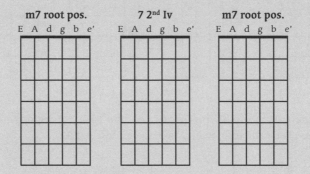

Sample chord progression: Dm7 – G7 – Cmaj7

⇨ Determine the root of Dm7 on the d–string and on the g–string (figure 245/246). Form the root position of the chord (12th /7th fret).

⇨ Determine the root of G7 on the A–string and on the d–string (figure 245/246). Form the 2nd inversion of the chord (10th/5th fret).

⇨ Determine the root of Cmaj7 on the d–string and on the g–string (figure 245/246). Form the root position of the chord (10th/5th fret)

⇨ Practice the chord progression on the strings A–d–g–b.

⇨ Practice the chord progression on the strings d–g–b–e'.

⇨ Transfer the fingerings into the following II – V – I progressions:
Am7 – D7 – Gmaj7
Cm7 – F7 – B♭maj7
Gm7 – C7 – Fmaj7

⇨ Practice the chord progressions on the strings A–d–g–b and d–g–b–e'.

Exercise 2

Our next exercise starts with the chord in its 2nd inversion:

[Figure 247: IIm7 – V7 – Imaj7 Drop2 voicings on the strings A–d–g–b]

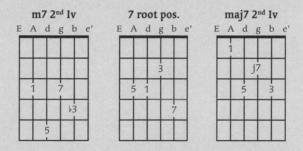

Task 8: Insert the voicings for the strings d–g–b–e' on your own. Start with the 2nd inversion.

[Figure 248: Task 8: IIm7 – V7 – Imaj7 Drop2 voicings on the strings d–g–b–e']

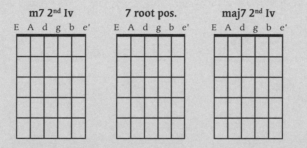

Sample chord progression: Dm7 – G7 – Cmaj7

⇨ Determine the root of Dm7 on the A–string and on the d–string (figure 247/248). Form the 2nd inversion of the chord (5th/12th fret).

⇨ Determine the root of G7 on the d–string and on the g–string (figure 247/248). Form the root position of the chord (5th/12th fret).

⇨ Determine the root of Cmaj7 on the A–string and on the d–string (figure 247/248). Form the 2nd inversion of the chord (3rd/10th fret).

⇨ Practice the chord progression on the strings A–d–g–b.

⇨ Practice the chord progression on the strings d–g–b–e'.

⇨ Transfer the fingerings into the following II – V – I progressions:
Am7 – D7 – Gmaj7
Cm7 – F7 – B♭maj7
Gm7 – C7 – Fmaj7

⇨ Practice the chord progressions on the strings A–d–g–b and d–g–b–e'.

Exercise 3

The following two exercises show minor II – V – I progressions. The first chord is in its root position.

[Figure 249: IIm7♭5 – V7 – Im7 Drop2 voicings on the strings A–d–g–b]

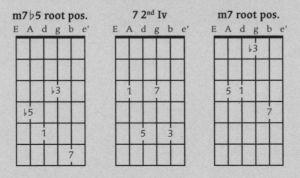

Task 9: Please insert the chord diagrams for the strings d–g–b–e' yourself.

[Figure 250: Task 9: IIm7♭5 – V7 – Im7 Drop2 voicings on the strings d–g–b–e']

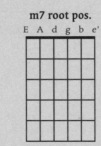

Sample chord progression: Em7♭5 – A7 – Dm7

- ⤸ Determine the root of Em7♭5 on the d–string and on the g–string (figure 249/250). Form the root position of the chord (14th/9th fret)

- ⤸ Determine the root of A7 on the A–string and on the d–string (figure 249/250). Form the 2nd inversion of the chord (12th/7th fret).

- ⤸ Determine the root of Dm7 on the d–string and on the g–string (figure 249/250). Form the root position of the chord (12th/7th fret).

- ⤸ Practice the chord progression on the strings A–d–g–b.

- ⤸ Practice the chord progression on the strings d–g–b–e'.

- ⤸ Transfer the fingerings into the following II – V – I progressions:
  F#m7♭5 – B7 – Em7
  Bm7♭5 – E7 – Am7
  Am7♭5 – D7 – Gm7

- ⤸ Practice the chord progressions on the strings A–d–g–b and d–g–b–e'.

Exercise 4

Now we start with the first chord in its 2nd inversion.

[Figure 251: IIm7♭5 – V7 – Im7 Drop2 voicings on the strings A–d–g–b]

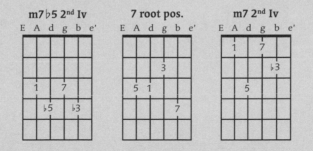

Task 10: Insert the chord diagrams for the strings d–g–b–e' yourself.

[Figure 252: Task 10: IIm7♭5 – V7 – Im7 Drop2 voicings on the strings d–g–b–e']

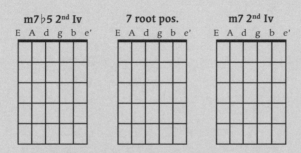

Sample chord progression: Em7♭5 – A7 – Dm7

⇨ Determine the root of Em7♭5 on the A–string and on the d–string (figure 251/252). Form the 2nd inversion of the chord (7th/14th fret).

⇨ Determine the root of A7 on the d–string and on the g–string (figure 251/252). Form the root position of the chord (7th/14th fret).

⇨ Determine the root of Dm7 on the A–string and on the d–string (figure 241/252). Form the 2nd inversion of the chord (5th/12th fret).

⇨ Practice the chord progression on the strings A–d–g–b.

⇨ Practice the chord progression on the strings d–g–b–e'.

⇨ Transfer the fingerings into the following II – V – I progressions:
F#m7♭5 – B7 – Em7
Bm7♭5 – E7 – Am7
Am7♭5 – D7 – Gm7

⇨ Practice the chord progressions on the strings A–d–g–b and d–g–b–e', too.

34-35

Exercise 5

Chord progression: Am7 – D7 – Gmaj7 – Cmaj7 – F#m7♭5 – B7 – Em7 – E7

↪ Start with the first chord in its root position. The next chord is formed in its 2nd inversion, and so on.

↪ Determine the roots of the chords. In root position, the root lies on the d–string. In 2nd inversion, you can find it on the A–string.

[Figure 253: Roots]

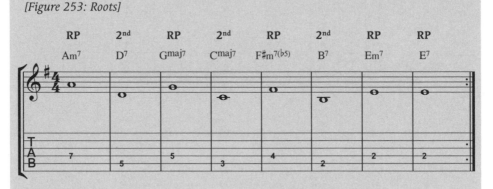

↪ Play the chord progression along with the playback (CD track: 34 slow; track 35: medium).

[Figure 254: Chord progression]

Repeat the exercise for the chord progressions in the following keys:

36/37
38/39
40/41

Dm7 – G7 – Cmaj7 – Fmaj7 – Bm7♭5 – E7 – Am7 – A7 [CD tracks 36/37]

Gm7 – C7 – Fmaj7 – B♭maj7 – Em7♭5 – A7 – Dm7 – D7 [CD tracks 38/39]

Cm7 – F7 – B♭maj7 – E♭maj7 – Am7♭5 – D7 – Gm7 – G7 [CD tracks 40/41]

Exercise 6
Chord progression: Am7 – D7 – Gmaj7 – Cmaj7 – F#m7♭5 – B7 – Em7 – E7

34-35

↪ Start with the first chord in its 2nd inversion. The next chord is formed in root position, and so on.

↪ Determine the roots of the chords. In 2nd inversion, the root lies on the A–string; in root position, you can find it on the d–string.

[Figure 255: Roots]

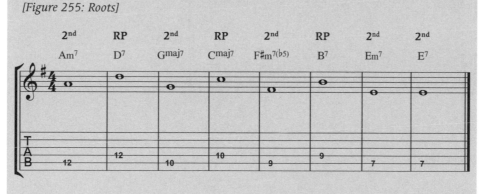

[Figure 256: Chord progression]

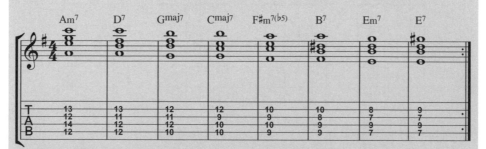

Repeat the exercise for the chord progressions in the following keys:
Dm7 – G7 – Cmaj7 – Fmaj7 – Bm7♭5 – E7 – Am7 – A7 [CD tracks 36/37]
Gm7 – C7 – Fmaj7 - B♭maj7 – Em7♭5 – A7 – Dm7 – D7 [CD tracks 38/39]
Cm7 – F7 - B♭maj7 – E♭maj7 – Am7♭5 – D7 – Gm7 – G7 [CD tracks 40/41]

36/37
38/39
40/41

Drop2 – 3rd inversion

In 3rd inversion, the fifth lies in the melody part. The third is set one octave lower and is in the bass.

[Figure 257: Drop2 Voicings in 3rd inversion (third in the bass)]

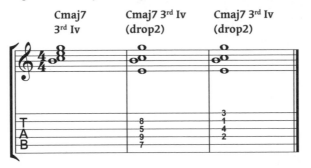

The following two figures present the voicings on the strings A–d–g–b and d–g–b–e':

[Figure 258: Drop2 voicings in 3rd inversion for the strings A–d–g–b]

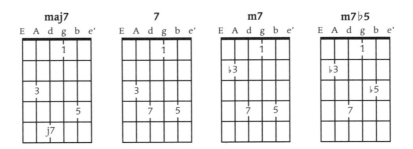

[Figure 259: Drop2 voicings in 3rd inversion for the strings d–g–b–e']

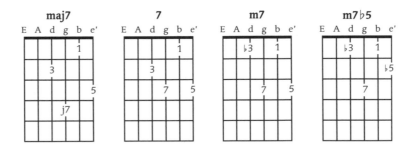

■ **Note:** In drop2 voicings in 3rd inversion, the fifth is in the melody part and the third lies in the bass. The seventh and the root form the middle parts.

Drop2 – 1st inversion

In the 1st inversion of a seventh chord in drop2, the root lies in the melody part, whereas the seventh is set one octave lower and lies in the bass.

[Figure 260: Drop2 Voicings in 1st inversion (seventh in the bass)]

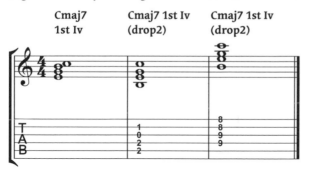

The following two figures present drop2 voicings in 1st inversion on the strings A–d–g–b and d–g–b–e':

[Figure 261: Drop2 voicings in 1st inversion for the strings A–d–g–b]

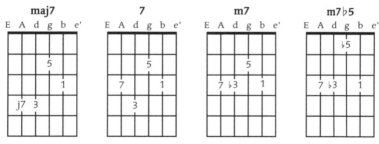

[Figure 262: Drop2 voicings in 1st inversion for the strings d–g–b–e']

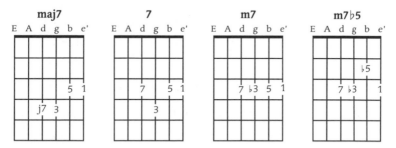

■ **Note:** In drop2 voicings in 1st inversion, the root is in the melody part and the seventh lies in the bass. The third and the fifth form the middle parts.

In close voicings, the positions of the chords of a cadence alternate. Therefore, if you start the cadence with a chord in its 3rd inversion, the next chord is built in 1st inversion, and vice versa.

Exercises on Drop2 Voicings in 1st and 3rd inversion

Exercise 1
I have compiled some exercises on the implementation of drop2 voicings in 3rd and 1st inversion, below. The exercises are based on major II–V–I progressions. We start with the first chord in its 3rd inversion.

[Figure 263: IIm7 – V7 – Imaj7 Drop2 voicings on the strings A–d–g–b]

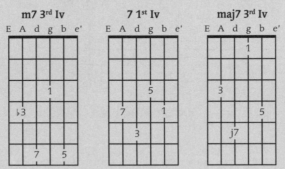

Task 11: Insert the voicings for the strings d–g–b–e' yourself. Start in 3rd inversion. You will find the solution in the appendix.

[Figure 264: Task 11: IIm7 – V7 – Imaj7 Drop2 voicings on the strings d–g–b–e']

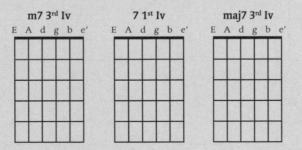

Sample chord progression: Dm7 – G7 – Cmaj7

⇨ Determine the root of Dm7 on the g–string and on the b–string (figure 263/264). Form the 3rd inversion of the chord (7th/3rdfret).

⇨ Determine the root of G7 on the b–string and on the e'–string (figure 263/264). Form the 1st inversion of the chord (8th/3rd fret).

⇨ Determine the root of Cmaj7 on the g–string and on the b–string (figure 263/264). Form the 3rd inversion of the chord (5th / 1st fret)

⇨ Practice the chord progression on the strings A–d–g–b.

⇨ Practice the chord progression on the strings d–g–b–e'.

⇨ Transfer the fingerings into the following II – V – I progressions:
  Am7 – D7 – Gmaj7
  Cm7 – F7 – B♭maj7
  Gm7 – C7 – Fmaj7

⇨ Practice the chord progressions on the strings A–d–g–b and d–g–b–e'.

Exercise 2
In the next exercise, we start in 1st inversion:

[Figure 265: IIm7 – V7 – Imaj7 Drop2 voicings on the strings A–d–g–b]

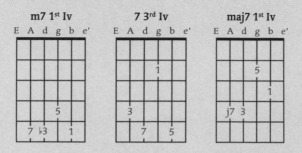

Task 12: Insert the voicings for the strings d–g–b–e' yourself. Start in 1st inversion.

[Figure 266: Task 12: IIm7 – V7 – Imaj7 Drop2 voicings on the strings d–g–b–e']

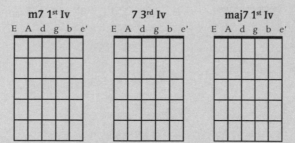

153

Sample chord progression: Dm7 – G7 – Cmaj7

↪ Determine the root of Dm7 on the b–string and on the e'–string (figure 265/266). Form the 1st inversion of the chord (3rd/10th fret).

↪ Determine the root of G7 on the g–string and on the b–string (figure 265/266). Form the 3rd inversion of the chord (open string/8th fret).

↪ Determine the root of Cmaj7 on the b–string and on the e'–string (figure 265/266). Form the 1st inversion of the chord (1st/8th fret).

↪ Practice the chord progression on the strings A–d–g–b.

↪ Practice the chord progression on the strings d–g–b–e'.

↪ Transfer the fingerings into the following II – V – I progressions:
Am7 – D7 – Gmaj7
Cm7 – F7 – B♭maj7
Gm7 – C7 – Fmaj7

↪ Practice the chord progressions on the strings A–d–g–b and d–g–b–e'.

Exercise 3
The following two exercises treat the change between the 3rd and 1st inversions in a minor II – V – I progression. We start in 3rd inversion.

[Figure 267: IIm7♭5 – V7 – Im7 Drop2 voicings on the strings A–d–g–b]

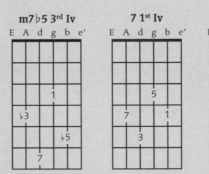

Task 13: Insert the voicings of the progression on the strings d–g–b–e' yourself. Start in 3rd inversion.

[Figure 268: Task 13: IIm7♭5 – V7 – Im7 Drop2 voicings on the strings d–g–b–e']

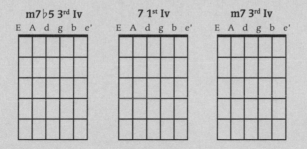

Sample chord progression: Em7♭5 – A7 – Dm7

↪ Determine the root of Em7♭5 on the g–string and on the b–string (figure 267/268). Form the 3rd inversion of the chord (9th/5th fret).

↪ Determine the root of A7 on the b–string and on the e'–string (figure267/268). Form the 1st inversion of the chord (10th/5th fret).

↪ Determine the root of Dm7 on the g–string and on the b–string (figure267/268). Form the 3rd inversion of the chord (7th/3rd fret).

↪ Practice the chord progression on the strings A–d–g–b.

↪ Practice the chord progression on the strings d–g–b–e'.

↪ Transfer the fingerings into the following II – V – I progressions:
F#m7♭5 – B7 – Em7
Bm7♭5 – E7 – Am7
Am7♭5 – D7 – Gm7

↪ Practice the chord progressions on the strings A–d–g–b and d–g–b–e'.

Exercise 4

Now start with the 1st inversion.

[Figure 269: IIm7♭5 – V7 – Im7 Drop2 voicings on the strings A–d–g–b]

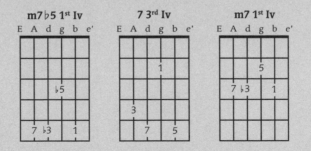

Task 14: Insert the voicings of the progression on the strings d–g–b–e' yourself. Start in 1st inversion.

[Figure 270: Task 14: IIm7♭5 – V7 – Im7 Drop2 voicings on the strings d–g–b–e']

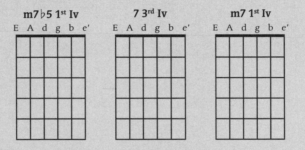

Sample chord progression: Em7♭5 – A7 – Dm7

⇨ Determine the root of Em7♭5 on the b–string and on the e'–string (figures 269/270). Form the 1st inversion of the chord (5th/12th fret)

⇨ Determine the root of A7 on the g–string and on the b–string (figures 269/270). Form the t3rd inversion of the chord (2nd/10th fret).

⇨ Determine the root of Dm7 on the b–string and on the e'–string (figures 269/270). Form the 1st inversion of the chord (3rd/10th fret).

⇨ Practice the chord progression on the strings A–d–g–b.

⇨ Practice the chord progression on the strings d–g–b–e'.

⇨ Transfer the fingerings into the following II – V – I progressions:
F#m7♭5 – B7 – Em7
Bm7♭5 – E7 – Am7
Am7♭5 – D7 – Gm7

⇨ Practice the chord progressions on the strings A–d–g–b and d–g–b–e'.

Exercise 5

Chord progression: Am7 – D7 – Gmaj7 – Cmaj7 – F#m7♭5 – B7 – Em7 – E7

▷ Start with the first chord in its 3rd inversion. The next chord is formed in 1st inversion, and so on.

▷ Determine the roots of the chords. In 3rd inversion, the root lies on the g–string; in 1st inversion, you'll find it on the b–string.

[Figure 271: Roots]

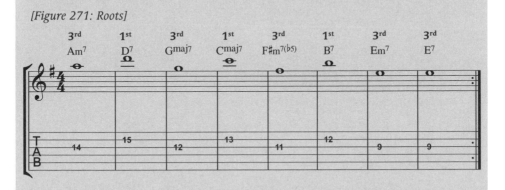

▷ Play the chord progression along with the playback (CD track 34: slow; track 35: medium).

[Figure 272: Chord progression]

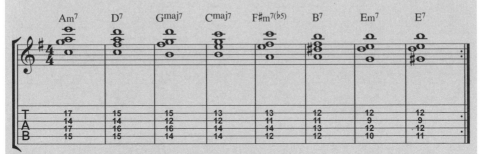

Repeat the exercise for the chord progressions in the following keys:

Dm7 – G7 – Cmaj7 – Fmaj7 – Bm7♭5 – E7 – Am7 – A7 [CD tracks 36/37]

Gm7 – C7 – Fmaj7 – B♭maj7 – Em7♭5 – A7 – Dm7 – D7 [CD tracks 38/39]

Cm7 – F7 – B♭maj7 – E♭maj7 – Am7♭5 – D7 – Gm7 – G7 [CD tracks 40/41]

Exercise 6
Chord progression: Am7 – D7 – Gmaj7 – Cmaj7 – F#m7♭5 – B7 – Em7 – E7

⇨ Start with the first chord in its 3rd inversion. The next chord is in its 1st inversion, and so on.

⇨ Determine the roots of the chords. In 3rd inversion, the root lies on the g–string. In 1st inversion, you'll find it on the b–string.

[Figure 273: Roots]

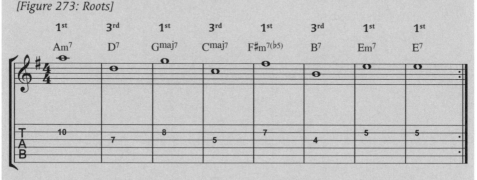

⇨ Play the chord progression along with the playback (CD track: 34 slow; track 35: medium).

[Figure 274: Chord progression]

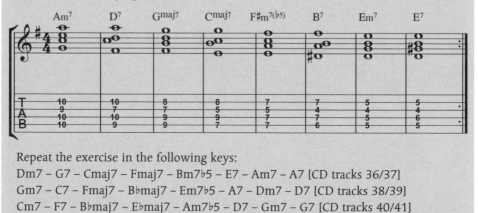

Repeat the exercise in the following keys:
Dm7 – G7 – Cmaj7 – Fmaj7 – Bm7♭5 – E7 – Am7 – A7 [CD tracks 36/37]
Gm7 – C7 – Fmaj7 – B♭maj7 – Em7♭5 – A7 – Dm7 – D7 [CD tracks 38/39]
Cm7 – F7 – B♭maj7 – E♭maj7 – Am7♭5 – D7 – Gm7 – G7 [CD tracks 40/41]

Of course, you can also combine the drop2 and drop3 voicings. With these quite extensive exercises, I wanted to show you how ideal voicings can be created with minimal shifts. As you can see in these exercises, in most cases, only two parts vary in the chord changes, whereas the remaining two parts stay the same. We have not treated drop4 voicings, because the resulting distribution of parts makes it impossible to play these voicings on the guitar.

10.3. Diminished 7th Chords

In the chapter about arpeggios on seventh chords, we focused on diminished 7th chords (dim7 or °7). Now, I would like to demonstrate the corresponding fingerings.

A C°7 chord consists of the notes c, eb, gb, bbb (to simplify matters, you can also imagine bbb as its enharmonic equivalent, a, which results from the double flattening of b).

You can implement °7 chords instead of dominant seventh chords or to harmonize off-scale notes of a melody. They create even more tension than a dominant 7th chord. Due to its symmetrical structure, you can easily shift this chord: after three frets, you get the identical chord in the corresponding inversion.

[Figure 275: C°7 drop3 voicings]

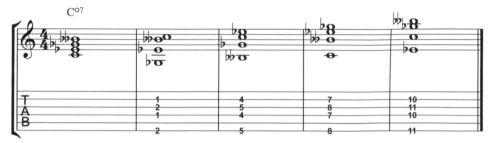

Of course, this is also the case for drop2 voicings, as you can see in figure 276.

[Figure 276: C°7 drop2 voicings]

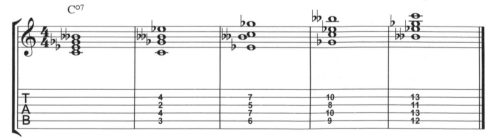

In figure 277, you see four relevant fingerings for the dim7 chord. The first two are presented as drop3 voicings, the others as drop2 voicings.

[Figure 277: °7 Voicings]

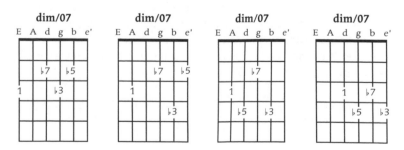

11.1. Ionian

Mode – many rock guitarists may at a loss at the mention of this term, and resign themselves to practicing power chords and playing in the pentatonic again. Often, this is due to complicated explanations or problems with the practical implementation. However, scarce knowledge about the fretboard is another factor. Let's approach the topic slowly.

The modes can be deduced from the major scale. If we play this scale from the root to the octave, then we've already heard the first mode. The mode of degree I is called Ionian (in our example, it is C major played from c to c'). In figure 278, we see the C major scale, or, from now on, the Ionian mode.

[Figure 278: Ionian]

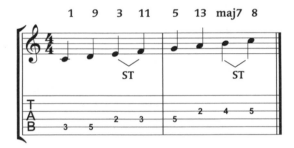

As mentioned before, you can find the semitone steps of the major scale between the 3rd/4th and 7th/8th notes. On the degree I, a C major chord or a Cmaj7 can be stacked. Some notes up to the seventh get their numbers from the first octave (root = 1, third = 3, fifth = 5, seventh = maj7). These notes build the so–called 'lower structure' of the corresponding chords. Other notes, that is, the second (9), fourth (11), and sixth (13) intervals derive their numbers from the second octave. In the group of optional notes, they are called 'upper structures'. Optional notes within a chord are not a 'must', but a 'can'. The fourth (11) especially has to be handled with care, as it creates a sus4 sound or strong friction which is not desirable most of the time. Identical chord types on different degrees have different optional notes.

The Ionian mode contains not only the triads and seventh chords as pointed out above, but also the optional major second (9), fourth (11), and major sixth (13). As we will see in the other modes, the construction of a major 7th chord plus the ninth, eleventh, and thirteenth can only be built once, namely on degree I of the major scale and is therefore typical of the Ionian mode.

We are going to deduce easy rules for the individual modes. This way, it will be easier to differentiate between them.

For the Ionian mode, we can state:

Triad:	major
seventh chord:	major 7th
Options:	9, 11, 13

Now we are going to combine triads and seventh chords with the arpeggios on seventh chords and add the optional notes of the corresponding mode. This way, we get the fingering of the scale. We tackle the fingering starting at the root and staying in the range of an octave. This means two or three strings per fretboard area remain unconsidered. However, I'd like to focus on the principles of the scale rather than covering each individual fretboard area.

We are going to divide the fingerings into five positions. Let's have a look at the first one.

[Figure 279: Ionian – Position 1]

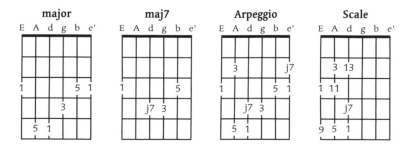

A short note on the structure:

The first image shows the triad of the position.
The second image shows the seventh chord of the position.
The third image shows the arpeggio on the seventh chord.
The fourth image shows the scale.

Try to memorize these four images. Together, they form a system which is going to be of great help for your later improvisations.

I have deliberately left out the notes on the high and low strings, as this could lead to confusion with each new mode we learn. When you feel that you are mastering the modes, you are welcome to fill in the gaps with your knowledge from the previous chapters.

Next, you see position 4 of the Ionian mode with the root on the A–string.

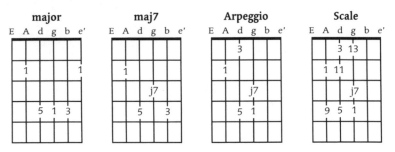

You already know the fingerings, and as you can see, the fingerings of the arpeggios and of the scale are identical to figure 279 (as expected), with the only difference being that they start on the A–string.

Figure 281 shows position 2 with the root on the d–string.

[Figure 281: Ionian – position 2]

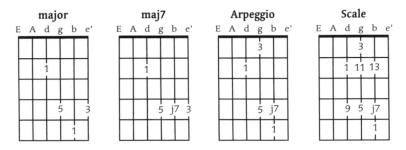

Of course, the fingerings for the b–string shift by one fret.

The next figure shows the Ionian mode in position 5. Here you see the fingering displayed progressively, according to the position. Thus, you start with the root on the g–string.

[Figure 282: Ionian – position 5]

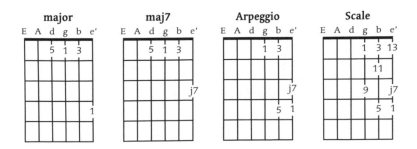

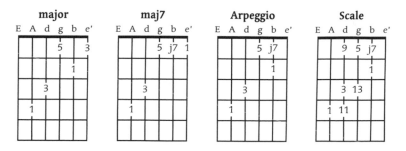

Using these five positions, you are now able to cover the Ionian mode on large areas of the fretboard. It's better that you understand the principles of the scale instead of being able to cover the complete fretboard.

Some modes sound more like major scales, others like minor scales. In order to carve out the individual differences, we are going to jump back and forth through the degrees of the major scale. Next in line is the mode of degree IV of the major scale: the Lydian mode.

11.2. Lydian

We get the Lydian mode by playing an ascending major scale, starting at the 4th note. For our exemplary key of C major, this would be from f to f'.

[Figure 284: F Lydian (IV. degree)]

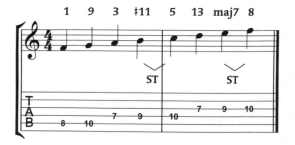

In the Lydian mode, the semitone steps are between the 4th/5th and the 7th/8th notes. From this, we can build a major triad and a maj 7th chord. Our fingerings and the arpeggio do not change. The only difference from the Ionian mode is the augmented fourth. The optional notes, 9 and 13, stay the same. Thus, you can imagine the Lydian scale as an Ionian scale with an augmented fourth (#11). This individual note confers a characteristic 'Lydian' sound.

For the Lydian mode, we can state:

Triad: Major
Seventh chord: major 7th
Options: 9, #11, 13

Let's have a look at the Lydian mode on the fretboard. The distribution of the four images is the same as in the previous chapter.

[Figure 285: Lydian – Position 1]

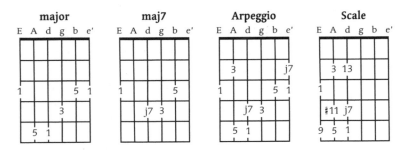

The first three images are analogous to the Ionian mode. Only the fourth image, the one with the scale, shows the change from the perfect fourth (Ionian) to the augmented fourth (#11). This is the specific interval for this mode and does not appear in any other mode of the major scale. Here you see the remaining four positions with the roots on the strings A, d, and g (figures 286–289).

[Figure 286: Lydian – Position 4]

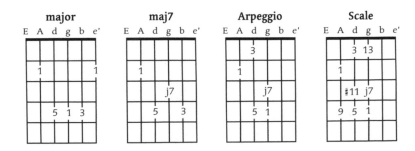

[Figure 287: Lydian – Position 2]

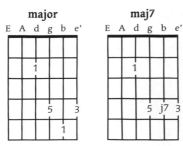

[Figure 288: Lydian – Position 5]

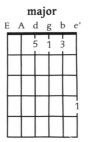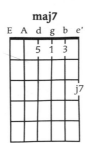

[Figure 289: Lydian – Position 3]

Next, we are going to have a look at the Mixolydian mode, which is built on degree V of the major scale.

11.3. Mixolydian

The Mixolydian mode results from degree V of the major scale, which is the note g in our case (fifth note in C major).
The semitone steps are between the 3rd/4th and the 6th/7th notes.

[Figure 290: Mixolydian (V. degree)]

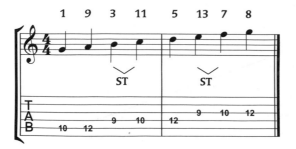

As you can see, only one note differs from the Ionian mode. However, the seventh chord also changes to a dominant 7th chord. We have already spoken about the effect of this chord and its striving for resolution into the tonic (see chapter 9.2). The optional notes are the same as in the Ionian mode.

For the Mixolydian mode, we can state:

Triad:	Major
Seventh chord:	dominant 7th
Options:	9, 11, 13

Here you can see the Mixolydian mode with its root on the E–string:

[Figure 291: Mixolydian – Position 1]

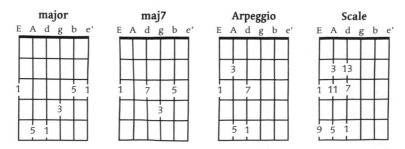

The difference from the Ionian mode becomes obvious in the second and third image. You can memorize the fingering of the Mixolydian scale as identical to the Ionian scale, but with a minor seventh. However, it is exactly this interval's characteristic which makes it harder for the Mixolydian scale to resolve into the octave, as the guide note is missing. Here you can see further fingerings and chords:

[Figure 292: Mixolydian – Position 4]

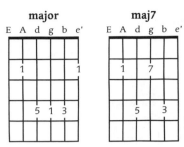

[Figure 293: Mixolydian – Position 2]

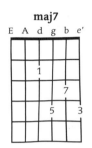

[Figure 294: Mixolydian – Position 5]

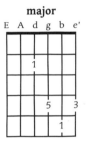

[Figure 295: Mixolydian – Position 3]

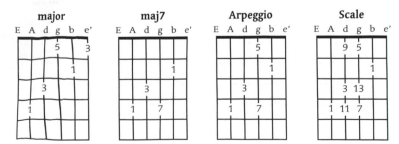

Let's proceed to the modes which most remind us of minor scales due to their minor third.

11.4. Aeolian

On degree VI of the major scale, the Aeolian mode (which we also know as the natural minor scale) can be built. For each major scale, there is a relative minor key. Both scales use the same tonal material, but start from different roots. The relative minor key of C major is A minor.

It is easy to determine the relative minor key of a corresponding major key on the fretboard: its root lies 3 frets lower (x–3) than the root of the major key. Of course, you can also determine the relative major scale, which lies three frets higher (x+3) than the root of the minor key. The semitone steps of the natural minor scale (Aeolian mode) are between the 2nd/3rd and the 5th/6th notes.

[Figure 296: Aeolian A (VI. degree)]

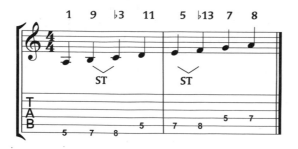

For the natural minor scale or the Aeolian mode, we can state:

Triad:	Minor
Seventh chord:	Minor 7th
Options:	9, 11, ♭13

[Figure 297: Aeolian – Position 1]

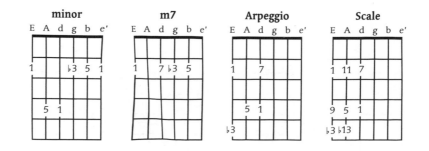

[Figure 298: Aeolian – Position 4]

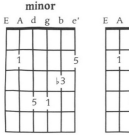

minor	m7	Arpeggio	Scale

[Figure 299: Aeolian – Position 2]

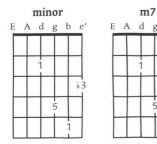

minor	m7	Arpeggio	Scale

[Figure 300: Aeolian – Position 5]

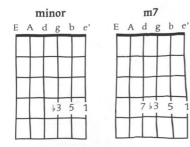

minor	m7	Arpeggio	Scale

[Figure 301: Aeolian – Position 3]

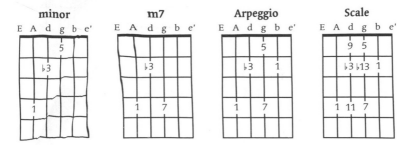

minor	m7	Arpeggio	Scale

In this chapter, we treat the natural minor scales predominantly as modes of the degree VI. Of course, in compositions, minor tonality is equally as important as major tonality. However, our aim is to get used to the timbre and sound of the diatonic modes.

11.5. Dorian

We get the Dorian mode by playing the notes of the major scale from the 2nd note up to its octave (degree II). Thus, the mode D Dorian is created by playing the C major scale from d to d'. Now, the semitone steps are between the 2nd/3rd and the 6th/7th notes. We can build a minor triad and a minor 7th chord. Due to its major sixth (13), the Dorian mode is also called the 'cheerful' minor.

[Figure 302: D Dorian (II. Degree)]

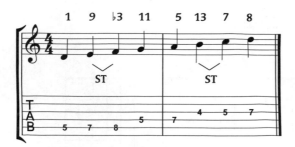

For the Dorian mode, we can state:

Triad:	Minor
Seventh chord:	Minor 7th
Options:	9, 11, 13

[Figure 303: Dorian – Position 1]

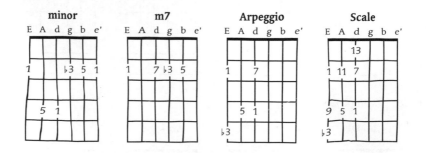

As the major sixth is the only difference between the Dorian and Aeolian modes, you only have to insert a major sixth instead of a minor sixth into the minor arpeggio.

[Figure 304: Dorian – Position 4]

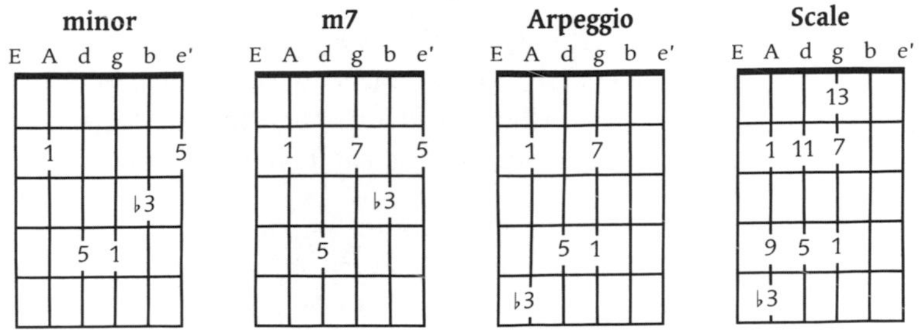

minor
E A d g b e'
m7
E A d g b e'
Arpeggio
E A d g b e'
Scale
E A d g b e'

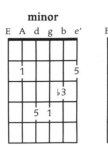

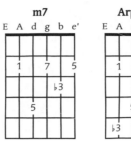

[Figure 305: Dorian – Position 2]

minor
E A d g b e'
m7
E A d g b e'
Arpeggio
E A d g b e'
Scale
E A d g b e'

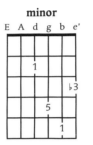

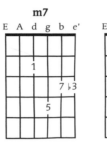

[Figure 306: Dorian – Position 5]

minor
E A d g b e'
m7
E A d g b e'
Arpeggio
E A d g b e'
Scale
E A d g b e'

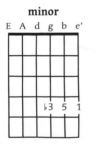

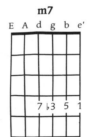

[Figure 307: Dorian – Position 3]

minor
E A d g b e'
m7
E A d g b e'
Arpeggio
E A d g b e'
Scale
E A d g b e'

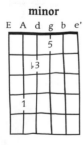

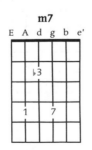

11.6. Phrygian

On degree III of the major scale, we obtain a minor sounding mode, namely the Phrygian mode. It only plays a small role in practical usage. Due to its semitone steps between the 1st/2nd and the 5th/6th notes, it creates the ♭9 and ♭13. The chord of degree III is seldom used in compositions, as the optional notes create great friction with root and fifth, respectively.

[Figure 308: E Phrygian (degree III)]

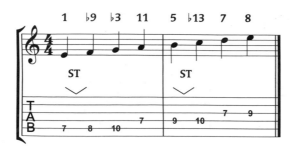

Thus, the difference to the Aeolian mode lies in the minor second. This is the easiest way to memorize the scale of the Phrygian mode.

For the Phrygian mode, we can state:

Triad:	Minor
Seventh chord:	Minor 7th
Options:	♭9, 11, ♭13

[Figure 309: Phrygian – Position 1]

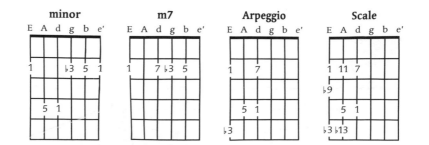

[Figure 310: Phrygian – Position 4]

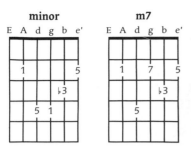
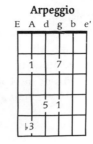

[Figure 311: Phrygian – Position 2]

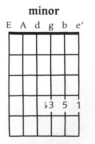
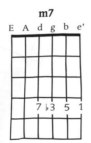

[Figure 312: Phrygian – Position 5]

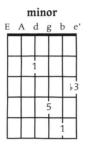
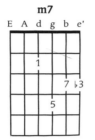

[Figure 313: Phrygian – Position 3]

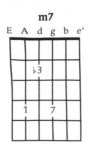

11.7. Locrian

The Locrian mode is built on degree VII of the major scale. This mode is scarcely used in a major context, but in a minor context it is very important as it can resume the function of the degree II. As an example, we can take the relative minor key of C major. In the natural A minor scale, a Bm7♭5 chord builds on degree II and brings in the material of the Locrian mode. The semitone steps of the Locrian mode are between the 1st/2nd and the 4th/5th notes. Optional notes are ♭9, 11, and ♭13. The diminished 5 (♭5) is diatonic!

For the Locrian mode, we can state:

Triad:	Diminished
Seventh chord:	minor7♭5 (half-diminished)
Options:	♭9, 11, ♭13

[Figure 314: B Locrian (VII. degree)]

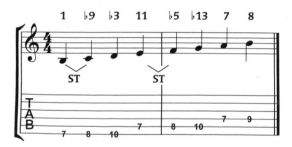

As there is a quite reasonable deviation between the Aeolian and the Locrian mode, you should not derive the fingerings for the Locrian mode. It is better to learn them as a separate system.

[Figure 315: Locrian – Position 1]

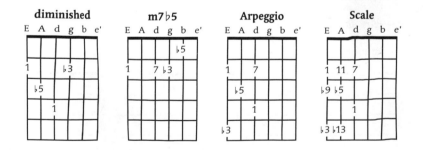

[Figure 316: Locrian – Position 4]

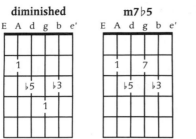

diminished	m7♭5	Arpeggio	Scale

[Figure 317: Locrian – Position 2]

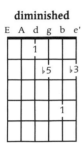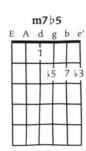

diminished	m7♭5	Arpeggio	Scale

[Figure 318: Locrian – Position 5]

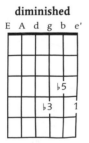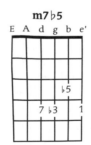

diminished	m7♭5	Arpeggio	Scale

[Figure 319: Locrian – Position 3]

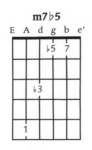

diminished	m7♭5	Arpeggio	Scale

11.8. The Jazz Cadence and Improvisation based on Modes

In order to create an improvisation over many types of chords, we have to study the jazz cadence. Here the subdominant, that is, degree IV of a key, is substituted by the minor chord of degree II. This process is also called 'minor substitution'. Quite frequently, dominant seventh chords are also substituted in jazz music.

This way, the classic IV – V – I progression changes to a II – V – I cadence. In jazz, chords usually consist of four notes. For C major, we get:

Classic Cadence:

F	G7	C
IV	V	I

Jazz Cadence:

Dm7	G7	Cmaj7
II	V	I

In order to harmonize the melody within this jazz cadence properly, you can use the Dorian mode for Dm7, the Mixolydian mode for G7, and the Ionian mode for Cmaj7:

Dm7	G7	Cmaj7
II	V	I
Dorian	Mixolydian	Ionian

The tonal centre of this progression is C major. If you are looking for the tonal centre of a phrase, make out the dominant seventh chord of the progression. As this chord only appears once in the respective key, you can identify it as the dominant. The following chord does not have to be the tonic chord: often, you are going to find an incomplete cadence, for example, a II – V progression without resolution into degree I, or a V – I progression without a preceding degree II. However, by finding the dominant, you can draw conclusions on the tonal centre.

This book predominantly treats II–V–I–IV progressions, which will benefit much of your playing. Another common chord progression is I–VI–II–V. The pertaining modes are: Ionian – Aeolian – Dorian – Mixolydian:

I	VI	II	V
Ionian	Aeolian	Dorian	Mixolydian

Jazz standards often change the tonal centre, which contributes to the charm of this type of music. But it also means that you will have to redefine the tonal centre quite often by working out degree V and deducing the pertaining modes. Unfortunately, there is no standard trick which can help to define each chord progression and to reduce the material to modes and keys.

CHAPTER 12

Excursion to Minor

12.1. Harmonic Minor

Music theory differentiates between three different minor keys. We have already treated the natural minor key in connection with the Aeolian mode (*see chapter 11.4*). If we build a II – V – I cadence within the natural A minor scale, we get the chord progression Bm7♭5 – Em7 – Am7. In the preceding chapters, we always have used a dominant 7th chord on degree V, as its major third resolves upwards into the root of the tonic. However, in the natural minor scale there is a whole tone step between the third of Em7 (g) and the root of Am7 (a). This means that there is no resolution due to the lack of the tritone friction we have in a conventional dominant 7th chord. This harmonic aspect was the trigger for developing the harmonic minor scale, where the seventh note is sharpened by a semitone. In our example, g becomes the guide note g#, and therefore, the Em7 chord (degree V in the natural minor) becomes an E7 chord (degree V in the harmonic minor).

This development also influences the sound of the scale considerably. Now, it contains semitone steps between the 2nd/3rd, 5th/6th, and 7th/8th notes. In addition, we get a step of three semitones between the 6th and the 7th notes. The harmonic minor scale sounds quite oriental to our ears. The chord on the first step is a minor^maj7th chord, which is rarely used.

[Figure 320: Harmonic Minor, A]

The basic arpeggio on a minor triad can now be extended by the optional notes 9, 11, ♭13. In order to build the scale, you can take the Aeolian mode (natural minor) and sharpen the seventh note.

For the harmonic minor scale, we can state:

Triad:	Minor
Seventh Chord:	minor^maj7th
Options:	9, 11, ♭13

[Figure 321: Harmonic minor in 4 positions]

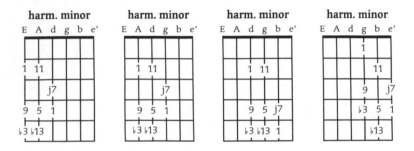

The harmonic minor scale is mostly used from its 5th note upwards. The resulting scale is called HM5 (harmonic minor degree V). In our example A harmonic minor, this is the scale E–HM5.

[Figure 322: The E–HM5 scale]

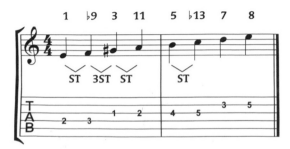

The HM5 scale is the most important scale for improvisations and melodies over degree V in a minor key, because we get a dominant 7th chord and the related options ♭9, 11, ♭13. When comparing this scale to the Mixolydian mode (the most important scale for improvisations over degree V in major progressions), we find that the only differences can be found in the options: we have 9 and 13 in the Mixolydian mode, but ♭9 and ♭13 in the HM5 scale.

For the HM5 scale, we can state:

Triad: Major
Seventh Chord: dominant 7th
Options: ♭9, 11, ♭13

[Figure 323: HM5 in 4 positions]

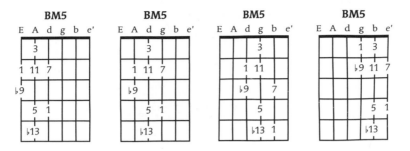

In order to avoid stretching, we place four notes on one string for the first time. It's best to master the resulting position change with a slide over one fret.

In notation, the dominant seventh chords for degree V of a minor scale contain the additional abbreviations ♭9 (for example, E7♭9, A7♭9) or ♭13. This refers to their function as a dominant 7th chord in a minor context. So, we play the Locrian, HM5 and Aeolian scales successively in a II – V – I progression. For example:

Degree:	IIm7♭5	V7♭9	Im7
Chord:	Bm7♭5	E7♭9	Am7
Scale:	B Locrian	E–HM5	A -Aeolian

[Figure 324: II – V – I Progression in A minor (starting point: B Locrian – position 4)]

Exercises on II7♭5 – V7♭9 – Im7

Here are two exercises with the tonal material treated above. Exercise 1 always starts with the root of the scale. In exercise 2, you start with the third.

[Figure 325: Exercise 1: II – V – I in minor]

[Figure 326: Exercise 2: II – V – I in minor]

Transfer these exercises to the remaining three positions of the corresponding modes and scales.

12. 2. Melodic Minor

Based on the harmonic minor scale, we build the melodic minor scale. As the augmented second between the 6th/7th notes sounds too oriental for classical music, the minor sixth has been sharpened to a major sixth. The resulting scale is called the 'melodic minor', as it has been created for melodic reasons. Its semitone steps are between the 2nd/3rd and the 7th/8th notes. Similar to the harmonic minor, a minormaj7th chord can be built. The optional notes are 9, 11, and 13. The fingering is easy to memorize: you play a major scale, but substitute the major third by a minor one, playing it one fret lower. Just like that, it becomes a melodic minor on the fretboard.

[Figure 327: A melodic minor]

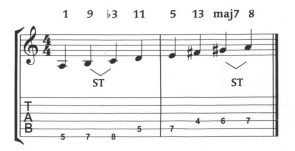

For the melodic minor scale, we can state:

Triad:	Minor
Seventh Chord:	minor^{maj7th}
Options:	9, 11, 13

[Figure 328: Melodic minor – 4 positions]

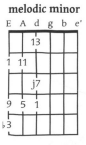

The melodic minor scale is predominantly used in modern jazz. The modes resulting from this scale are a treasure chest for jazz musicians and friends of new material. Especially interesting is degree VII of the melodic minor scale. Let's take F melodic minor and play the scale from e to e'. This scale is called the 'altered e'.

[Figure 329: Altered E – Derived from F melodic minor]

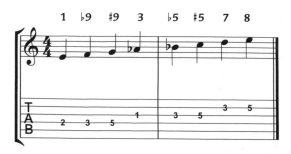

Start by playing the 1st, 4th, and 7th notes of the scale. You get the arpeggio of a dominant 7th chord without the fifth. Thus, an altered chord is a kind of dominant seventh chord. The alteration refers to the fifth and to the optional notes of 9 and 11.

Now, we apply the notes of the scale we have not yet played to the functions 5, 9, and 11. We have identified the 4th note as the major third (enharmonic: g#). The 2nd note of the scale, f, is the optional ♭9. The 3rd note can be treated as an augmented second f##, which corresponds to the optional #9. The 5th note (a♭) is six semitones steps away from the root and therefore corresponds to the optional ♭5. The 6th note can be enharmonically changed to b#, which is the optional #5.

What results is the dominant 7th chord, the fifth of which can be played as diminished (♭5) or augmented (#5). The same is true for the optional 9, which can be flat (♭9) or sharp (#9). Here is the scale with the correct harmonic representation of the notes:

[Figure 330: E altered – with correct optional notes]

In the following figure, you see the fingerings of the altered scale within an octave. Unfortunately, it is not possible to play the scale in one position without over–stretching.

For the altered scale, we can state:

Triad: augmented
Seventh chord: dominant 7th
Options: b9, #9, b5, #5

[Figure 331: Altered in 4 positions]

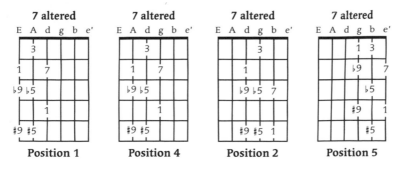

The altered scale is a dominant seventh scale which is mostly used in mode changes (mc). This expression describes the change from major to minor and vice versa within a cadence. Let's take a II – V – I progression as an example:

Bm7b5 – E7b9 – Am7

Now we replace degree I with the corresponding major 7th chord. The dominant 7th chord of degree V is now played as an altered chord ("alt"). The chord progression is now:
Bm7b5 – E7alt – Amaj7

The material for improvisations is now B Locrian (II), E altered (V) – A Ionian (I).

The same is true when we replace the first chord of the original cadence by a minor 7th chord, which is the degree II in the major:

Bm7b5 – E7b9 – Am7 ⇨ Bm7 – E7alt – Am7
Our tonal material for improvisations is now B Dorian – E altered – A Aeolian.

The altered scale is very important in jazz music, therefore, practice it well. It is also used in so–called 'inside – outside' improvisational concepts, where you leave the diatonic sound in order to create an interesting new sound. For example, you can use an altered scale over a dominant 7th chord; when you hit the tonic again, you come back to the diatonic mode.

Exercise

Here are two exercises which connect these scales in a mode change.

[CD 42, Figure 332: II – V – I progression with mode change to major]

[CD 43, Figure 333: II – V – I progression with mode change to minor]

12.3 Summary of the Scales and Exercises

[Figure 334: Summary of the scales and modes in intervals]

Scale	Chord	Intervals						
Ionian	Major7th	1	9	3	11	5	13	maj7
Dorian	Minor7th	1	9	♭3	11	5	13	7
Phrygian	Minor7th	1	♭9	♭3	11	5	♭13	7
Lydian	Major7th	1	9	3	#11	5	13	maj7
Mixolydian	Dominant7th	1	9	3	11	5	13	7
Aeolian	Minor7th	1	9	♭3	11	5	♭13	7
Locrian	Minor7th♭5	1	♭9	♭3	11	♭5	♭13	7
Harmonic Minor	Minor maj7th	1	9	♭3	11	5	♭13	maj7
HM5	Dominant7th♭9	1	♭9	3	11	5	♭13	7
Melodic Minor	Minor maj7th	1	9	♭3	11	5	13	maj7
Altered	7♭9♭5/#9#5	1	♭9	#9	3	♭5	#5	7

Memorize these chords, arpeggios and options well. They are the key to enhancing your improvisations and melodies. Of course, there are even more scales and modes, but with the ones we have treated here, you should have enough to attempt jazz improvisation. You can study all further scales with the help of a good manual about jazz harmony. You can always integrate new scales into the interval and arpeggio schemes of the last chapters.

In order to conclude this chapter about modes and scales, I would like to equip you with some exercises on jazz cadences. Practice them in all four positions, and you will make huge progress. Of course, you can also insert the modes into improvisations over rock and pop songs you know.

Exercises on the Modes

■ **Note:** The chord of the 8th bar is the dominant which leads back to the beginning. This kind of dominant is called secondary dominant. As the target chord is Am7, we use the E HM5 scale for E7♭9.

34-41

[Figure 335: Exercise on the Modes]

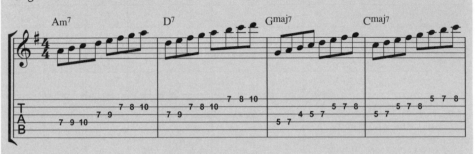

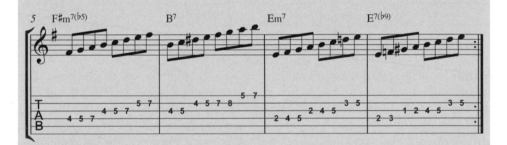

↳ Choose one of the rhythm patterns of figure 336.

↳ Play this pattern with the scale pertaining to the chord (see figure 335).

↳ Start the pattern on the root of the chord.

↳ Start the pattern on the third of the chord.

↳ Start the pattern on the fifth of the chord.

↳ Start the pattern on the seventh of the chord.

↳ Play ascending and descending lines.

↳ Vary the positions.

↳ And create your own rhythm patterns!

34-41

CHAPTER 13

Seventh Chords with Options

Finally, we are going to learn how to integrate optional notes into seventh chords. Here, anything goes, or rather anything that is feasible within the corresponding mode or scale. Metaphorically speaking, options in chords are not that different from painting. Optional notes are the tone colors you can add to basic chords.

We have treated the fourth as an optional note (4 or 11). In practical usage, its implementation is quite dangerous as it suggests a suspension and creates friction with the major thirds of the maj7th and dominant 7th chords. However, in m7th chords, the 11 creates a great sound. The ninth (9) and thirteenth (13) and their alterations are the optional notes we use the most. There is a great variety of options for implementing the dominant 7th in particular.

First, let's have a look at major 7th chords. Here, the optional note 13 can be integrated best into the 3rd inversion of the drop3 voicing. We substitute the fifth for the sixth (13). As the fifth is the same except for the group of diminished chords, it is not strictly necessary for the quality of the seventh chord.

For 9-chords, the octave of the root is sharpened by a semitone or whole tone. Generally, it is possible to add optional notes to every major 7th chord you already know. If there is no other option, replace the root by the second (9) or the fifth by the sixth (13). When you replace the root, the bass player should play it in order to define the key.

[Figure 337: Major 7th chords with options]

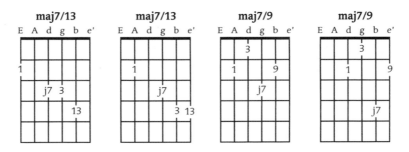

In dominant 7th chords, drop3 voicings in 3rd inversion are perfectly suited to additions and variations of the fifth (dim/aug). The options #9, ♭5 and #5 suggest altered dominant 7th chords.

[Figure 338: Dominant 7th chords with additions 13 and #5 (♭13)]

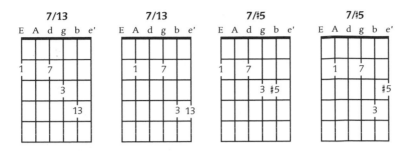

[Figure 339: Dominant 7th chords with additions ♭5 and #9]

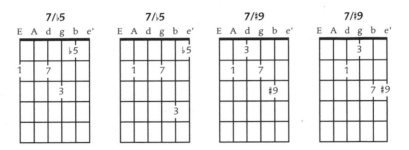

The option 9 points to a degree V in the major keys, and ♭9 often points to a degree V in minor keys.

[Figure 340: Dominant 7th chords with additions 9 and ♭9]

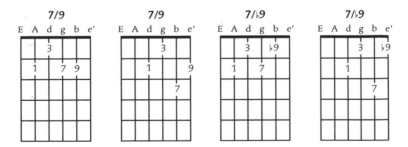

For the minor 7th chords, here are some chord diagrams for the chords with 9 and 11.

[Figure 341: Minor 7th chords with the addition 9]

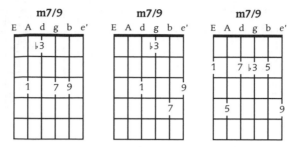

[Figure 342: Minor 7th chords with the addition 11]

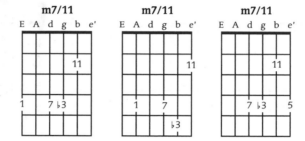

Finally, here are two examples with extended chords. Pay attention to the voicings and the great sounds which result from them. This is only to be regarded as a way in, as there are many more ways to create and implement chords with options than can possibly be shown here. Nevertheless, now you have the know-how you need to create such chords on your own!

Have fun traveling through the sounds!

[Figure 343: Exercise on chords with options in A major / F#m]

[Figure 344: Exercise on chords with options in G major / Em]

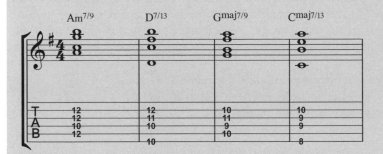

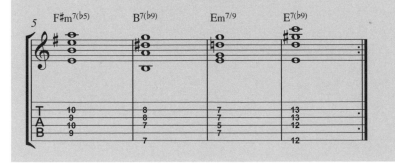

CD Index and Descriptions of the Exercises

Track 1: Audio sample riff A major (Figure 109)
Track 2: Audio sample riff A major (Figure 110)
Track 3: Audio sample riff A major (Figure 111)
Track 4: Audio sample riff Asus4 (Figure 131)
Track 5: Audio sample picking A – sus4 – sus2 (Figure 133)
Track 6: Audio sample riff C major (Figure 135)
Track 7: Audio sample funk rock with sixths (Figure 154)

Track 8: Exercise on major arpeggios (Figures 64 and 68) with 54 bpm

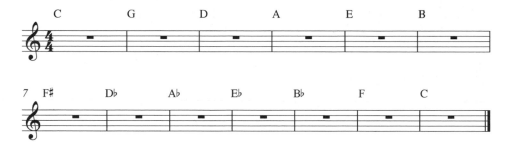

Play the major arpeggios in one position for the corresponding chord and follow the instructions of figures 64 to 68. In the three following tracks, the tempo increases steadily. In a similar way, practice the arpeggios for minor (track 12 – 15), diminished (track 16 - 19) and augmented (track 20 – 23) chords.

Track 9: Exercises on major arpeggios (figures 64 and 68), 66 bpm
Track 10: Exercises on major arpeggios (figures 64 and 68), 78 bpm
Track 11: Exercises on major arpeggios (figures 64 and 68), 90 bpm

Track 12: Exercises on minor arpeggios (figure 65), 54 bpm

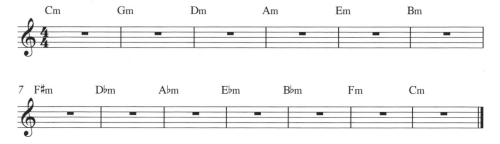

Track 13: Exercises on minor arpeggios (figure 65), 66 bpm
Track 14: Exercises on minor arpeggios (figure 65), 78 bpm
Track 15: Exercises on minor arpeggios (figure 65), 90 bpm

Track 16: Exercises on diminished arpeggios (figure 66), 54 bpm

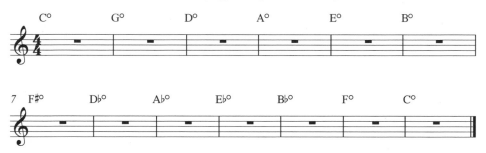

Track 17: Exercises on diminished arpeggios (figure 66), 66 bpm
Track 18: Exercises on diminished arpeggios (figure 66), 78 bpm
Track 19: Exercises on diminished arpeggios (figure 66), 90 bpm

Track 20: Exercises on augmented arpeggios (figure 67), 54 bpm

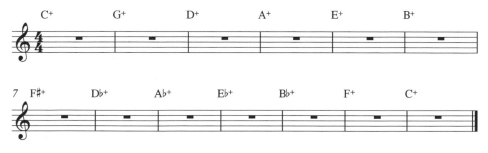

Track 21: Exercises on augmented arpeggios (figure 67), 66 bpm
Track 22: Exercises on augmented arpeggios (figure 67), 78 bpm
Track 23: Exercises on augmented arpeggios (figure 67), 90 bpm

Track 24: Exercises on the major classic cadence in the circle of fifths (figure 87), 60 bpm

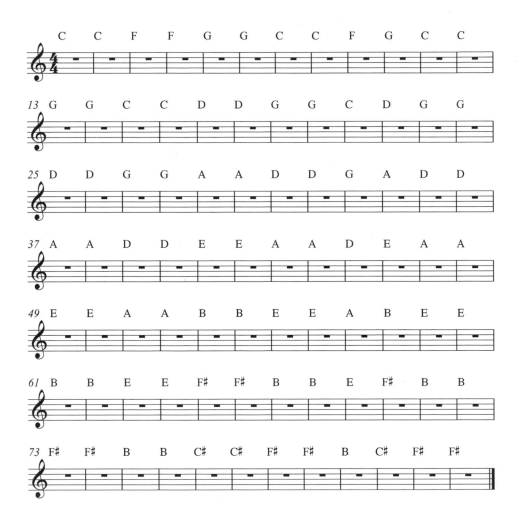

Practice the cadence for all keys, starting from one position. On the playback, you hear two measures of each degree of the cadence with a one measure change, which gives you enough time to practice. Afterwards, the playback changes to the next key. Now, shift the root of the position to the new key. This way, you will learn to use the positions and fingerings in all keys.

Repeat this procedure for track 25, which treats the major cadences of the circle of fourths.

Track 25: Exercises on the major classic cadence in the circle of fourths (figure 87), 72 bpm

Track 26: Exercises on the major classic cadence in the circle of fifths (figure 91), 60 bpm

You can practice the minor classic cadences with track 26 (circle of fifths) and track 27 (circle of fourths) in the same way as the major cadence. You will find the corresponding positions in figure 91.

| Am | Am | Dm | Dm | E | E | Am | Am | Dm | E | Am | Am |

13 Em Em Am Am B B Em Em Am B Em Em

25 Bm Bm Em Em F♯ F♯ Bm Bm Em F♯ Bm Bm

37 F♯m F♯m Bm Bm C♯ C♯ F♯m F♯m Bm C♯ F♯m F♯m

49 C♯m C♯m F♯m F♯m G♯ G♯ C♯m C♯m F♯m G♯ C♯m C♯m

61 G♯m G♯m C♯m C♯m D♯ D♯ G♯m G♯m C♯m D♯ G♯m G♯m

73 D♯m D♯m G♯m G♯m A♯ A♯ D♯m D♯m G♯m A♯ D♯m D♯m

Track 27: Exercises on the minor classic cadence in the circle of fourths (figure 91), 72 bpm

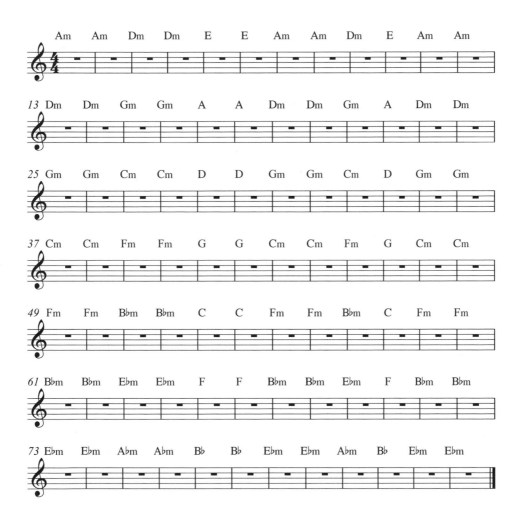

Track 28: Exercises on arpeggios on triads (figures 93 and 94)

Here you can practice the arpeggios on the triads with the pattern from figure 93. Also create your own patterns for your improvisation. Tracks 29 and 30, give two further backing tracks in other keys and styles.

Track 29: Exercises on arpeggios on triads (figures 93 and 94)

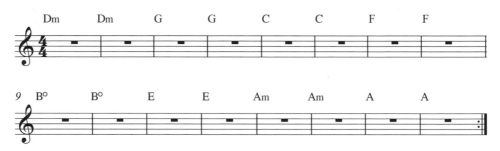

Track 30: Exercises on arpeggios on triads (figures 93 and 94)

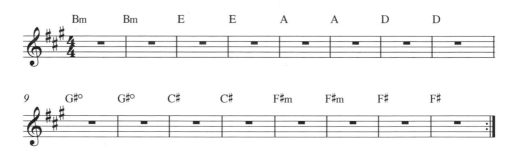

Track 31: Exercises on voicings on triads (figures 102 to 104)

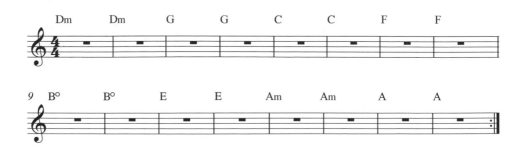

Here you can practice the voicings from figure 104. Use the sequence of root position and 1st/2nd inversion. Create and vary your own rhythm patterns!

The chord progressions in tracks 32 and 33 are available in different keys and styles.

Track 32: Exercises on voicings on triads (figures 102 to 104)

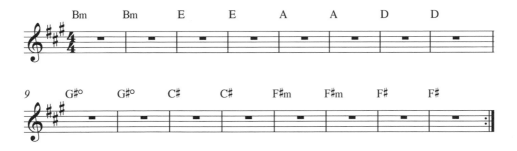

Track 33: Exercises on voicings on triads (figures 102 to 104)

Track 34: Exercises on four–note chords and scales (chapters 9–13), 116 bpm

With tracks 34 to 41, you can practice the contents of chapters 9–13. These tracks are recorded without guitar. Here, you can try the voicings of the seventh chords (drop2, drop3, extended chords).

You can also use these tracks to practice arpeggios and modes. Be careful to use the correct mode! Here, figures 307 and 308 can help you.

The first four measures represent a major II–V–I–IV progression. The correct succession of the modes is A Dorian, D Mixolydian, G Ionian and C Lydian. Measures 5–7 represent a minor II – V – I progression. The material for improvisations is: F# Locrian, B–HM5 and E Aeolian.

The 8th measure is the dominant which leads back to the beginning. Here, you can use E HM5 or E altered.

The tracks of a progression are recorded at two different speeds, so, start with the slower version.

Track 35: Exercises on four-note chords and scales (chapters 9–13) – 154 bpm

Track 36: Exercises on four–note chords and scales (chapters 9–13) – 116 bpm

Track 37: Exercises on four–note chords and scales (chapters 9–13) – 154 bpm

Track 38: Exercises on four–note chords and scales (chapters 9–13) – 116 bpm

Track 39: Exercises on four–note chords and scales (chapters 9–13) – 154 bpm

Track 40: Exercises on four–note chords and scales (chapters 9–13) – 116 bpm

Track 41: Exercises on four–note chords and scales (chapters 9–13) – 154 bpm

Track 42: II–V–I mode change to major (figure 302)

Track 43: II–V–I mode change to minor (figure 303)

Solutions: Chapters 10.1 and 10.2

Task 1 (figure 214)

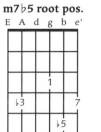

m7♭5 root pos. — E A d g b e'

7 2nd Iv — E A d g b e'

m7 root pos. — E A d g b e'

Task 2 (figure 216)

m7♭5 2nd Iv — E A d g b e'

7 root pos. — E A d g b e'

m7 2nd Iv — E A d g b e'

Task 3 (figure 228)

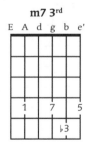

m7 3rd — E A d g b e'

7 1st Iv — E A d g b e'

maj7 3rd Iv — E A d g b e'

Task 4 (figure 230)

m7 1st Iv — E A d g b e'

7 3rd Iv — E A d g b e'

maj7 1st Iv — E A d g b e'

Task 5 (figure 232)

| m7♭5 3rd Iv | 7 1st Iv | m7 3rd |

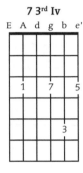

Task 6 (figure 234)

| m7♭5 1st Iv | 7 3rd Iv | m7 1st Iv |

Task 7 (figure 246)

| m7 root pos. | 7 2nd Iv | maj7 root pos. |

Task 8 (figure 248)

| m7 2nd Iv | 7 root pos. | maj7 2nd Iv |

Task 9 (figure 250)

m7♭5 root pos.
E A d g b e'

		♭5	♭3		
			1		
					7

7 2nd Iv
E A d g b e'

			1		
				7	
				5	3

m7 root pos.
E A d g b e'

				♭3	
			5	1	
					7

Task 10 (figure 252)

m7♭5 2nd Iv
E A d g b e'

	1				
		♭5	7	♭3	

7 root pos.
E A d g b e'

	5	1	3		
				7	

m7 2nd Iv
E A d g b e'

			1		
				7	♭3
		5			

Task 11 (figure 264)

m7 3rd
E A d g b e'

		♭3	1		
			7	5	

7 1st Iv
E A d g b e'

		7		5	1
			3		

maj7 3rd Iv
E A d g b e'

					1
			3		
					5
			j7		

Task 12 (figure 266)

m7 1st Iv
E A d g b e'

		7	♭3	5	1

7 3rd Iv
E A d g b e'

				1	
	3				
			7		5

maj7 1st Iv
E A d g b e'

				5	1
		j7	3		

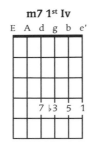

Task 13 (figure 268)

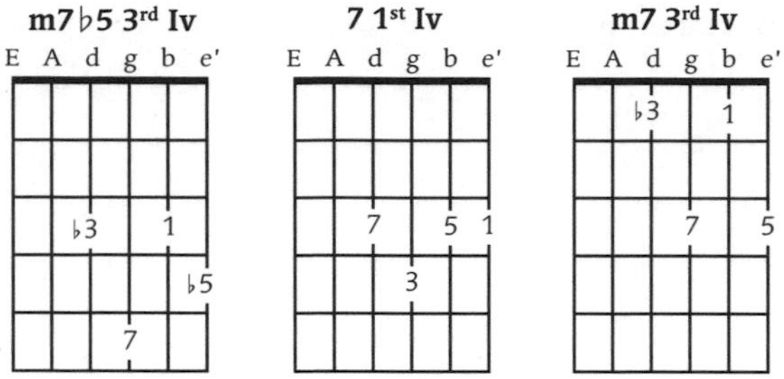

m7♭5 3rd Iv

E A d g b e'
	♭3	1	
			♭5
	7		

7 1st Iv

E A d g b e'
	7	5 1	
	3		

m7 3rd Iv

E A d g b e'
		♭3	1
		7	5

Task 14 (figure 270)

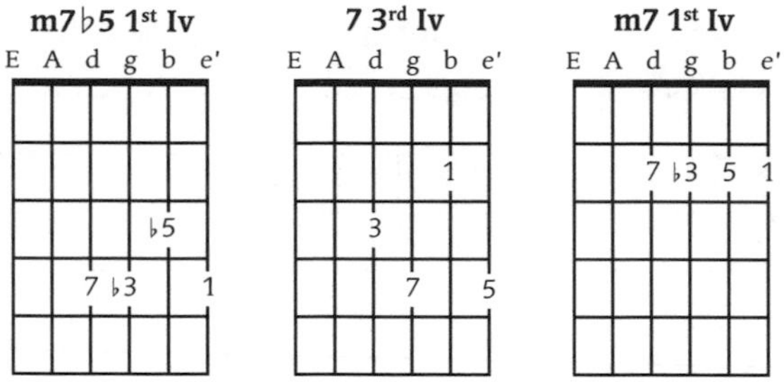

m7♭5 1st Iv

E A d g b e'
		♭5	
	7 ♭3	1

7 3rd Iv

E A d g b e'
			1
	3		
		7	5

m7 1st Iv

E A d g b e'
		7 ♭3 5 1

204

Quotations of Themes

1) Fear Of The Dark (Iron Maiden)
Music/Text: Stephen Percy Harris
Original Publisher (OP): Iron–Maiden–Publishing Overseas Ltd

2) Last Resort (Papa Roach)
Music/Text: David J. Buchner, Tobin Joseph Esperance, Jerry Allan Horton Jr., Jacoby Dokota Shaddix
OP: BMG Rights Management (Ireland) Limited
Viva La Cucaracha Music

3) Crazy Train (Ozzy Osbourne)
Music/Text: John Osbourne, Robert John Daisley, Randy Rhoads
OP: Aviation Music LTD
Blizzard Music LTD

4) Summer of ´69 (Bryan Adams)
Music/Text: Bryan Guy Adams, Jim Vallance
OP: Adams Communications Inc., Irving Music, Almo Music Corporation, Testatyme Music

5) Every Breath You Take (The Police)
Music/Text: Gordon Matthew Sumner
OP: GM Sumner

6) The Sound Of Silence (Simon & Garfunkel)
Music/Text: Paul Simon
OP: Paul Simon Music

7) Autumn Leaves
Music/Text: Joseph Kosma, Jacques Charles Enoch, Jacques Prévert
OP: Enoch and cie
Morky–Music Co. Inc.

8) Belief (John Mayer)
Music/Text: John Mayer
OP: Goodium Music Inc

Acknowledgements

Finally, I would like to express my gratitude to those who have supported me and the publication of this book considerably.

First, I would like to thank my wife Manuela, and my children Laura and Marco. A musician's job is not a nine-to-five day. Nevertheless, they always stand by me, even though I have spent so much time on the computer writing this book, in addition to concerts and classes. I love you.

My thanks also to:

Nico Schellhammer and Julia Baldauf at Schott Music, who have helped me to realize my plans. Whenever a problem arose, they solved it.

Ingrid Baumann. Ingrid translated my book into English. Her calm and considerate ways helped me greatly in managing the necessary adaptations for the English version of this book, and she always met my requests.

Stefan Weber and Dario Mischke. They both have familiarized themselves with the content of the book in order to propose English definitions and technical terms.

My expert editor Helmut Kagerer, who helped me to make the German original consistent.

My studio crew, Christoph Raba (recording), Tobias Meier (bass), and Dominic Jordans (drums) for their participation on the accompanying CD.

Anna Pöller for the photo on the back cover.

Phil X, Devin Townsend, Phil Campbell and Stevie Salas for the kind testimonials and words about this book.

Marcus Spangler from Warwick/Framus for his friendship and help.

Dr Bernhard Schönhärl for the medical supervision during the hard times during which this book came into existence.

Laney Amplification (James Laney, Roger Williams) and Tom Weise from Laney Germany for the great support and the friendship. Laney Amps rock!!!

G&L Guitars and Frank Fügner from Musik Wein for the wonderful G&L guitars.

Gerhard Schwarz from Schwarz Custom Guitars for my great Custom Strat.

Martin Kürzinger and all my colleagues from the ESR Parsberg and the Musikwerkstatt Frauenberg.

Last but not least, thanks to all my students, who work ambitiously to uphold the magic of the guitar.